THE CHEERS
AND THE TEARS

THE CHEERS AND THE TEARS

A Healthy Alternative to the Dark Side of Youth Sports Today

Shane Murphy, Ph.D.

Jossey-Bass Publishers
San Francisco

Jossey-Bass books and products are available through most bookstores. To contact Jossey-Bass directly, call (888) 378-2537, fax to (800) 605-2665, or visit our website at www.josseybass.com.

Substantial discounts on bulk quantities of Jossey-Bass books are available to corporations, professional associations, and other organizations. For details and discount information, contact the special sales department at Jossey-Bass.

 Manufactured in the United States of America on Lyons Falls Turin Book. This paper is acid-free and 100 percent totally chlorine-free.

Library of Congress Cataloging-in-Publication Data

Murphy, Shane M., 1957–
    The cheers and the tears: a healthy alternative to the dark side of youth sports today/Shane Murphy.—1st ed.
        p. cm.
    Includes bibliographical references and index.
    ISBN 0-7879-4037-2 (cloth: acid-free paper)
    1. Sports for children—United States. 2. Sports for children—Social aspects—United States. I. Title.
    GV709.2 .M873 1999
    796'.083'0973—ddc21

                                                                            98-25525

FIRST EDITION
PB Printing   10 9 8 7 6 5 4 3 2 1

CONTENTS

To Annemarie,
the true north of my life's compass

ACKNOWLEDGMENTS

Thanks to Alan Rinzler at Jossey-Bass, who was supportive of my idea for a book that would take an honest look at children's sports and who motivated me throughout the difficult process of writing it.

Many thanks to my colleagues who gave of their time and energy to discuss these issues, especially: Sean McCann, who helped me get the ball rolling; Jay Coakley, whose work and depth of thinking on these issues I greatly admire; Othon "Sam" Kesend, whose research approach to this topic was ahead of its time; Renee Parker, who gave me valuable feedback on the manuscript; and Tara Scanlan, who has generously shared her thoughts with me over the years.

I owe a great deal to my Mum and Dad, who exposed me to many sports through their own active participation. My father had a huge influence on me through the just and enthusiastic way he handled being a youth sport coach.

And my love and gratitude to my wife, Annemarie, and my children, Bryan and Theresa. I can't tell you how much I love you.

Trumbull, Connecticut   Shane Murphy
December 1998

INTRODUCTION

I love being involved in youth sports. I love the fun that children have playing their favorite games, the way that youth sports can bring families together, and the way that sports can teach children wonderful lessons about teamwork, setting goals, and the value of hard work.

I hate being involved in youth sports. I hurt when a thirteen-year-old athlete sits down with me and tells me how much she dislikes all the practice she is doing, how she would rather be doing something else, but how she doesn't want to tell her parents and hurt their feelings. I become angry when I see parents on the sidelines screaming at their kids, making everyone around them uncomfortable and ruining the experience for their children. I get sick when I hear about the latest episode of violence in youth sports—a parent punching an official, a coach shoving a child, parents fighting in the stands.

I'm standing on the sidelines at John Q. Yancy Park in Fairfield County, Connecticut, on a blustery Saturday morning in the fall. Five soccer fields are laid out in the park, and more than a hundred young children mill around, happily playing soccer. Nearly that many parents are watching with me from the sidelines. With the athletes' brightly colored uniforms, the shouts from parents, the blasts from the whistles of the officials, and the yelling of the children, it's a colorful and noisy spectacle. The experience embodies my ambiguity about youth sports.

It seems that most of the people here are having fun. But as one game ends, a father walks over to his young son, who can't be even ten years old, and begins yelling at him for missing a penalty kick. "How many times did we work on that in practice?" the man yells, growing red in the face. "You don't care, do you? Why can't you try? This might be your last game, fella!" The child walks beside him, head down and tears streaming down his face. I watch and listen unwillingly. I'd like to go up to this abusive father and give him a piece of my mind, but I realize I would probably make the situation worse. Other parents nearby also look uncomfortable, until the father and son disappear into the adjacent parking lot.

Aren't youth sports supposed to be about having fun? Yes, but today youth sports are about much more than fun. They have become part of a big business, and the sheer numbers of young Americans involved (at least twenty million children between five and thirteen participate in organized sports programs) give us pause to consider. Why are youth sports programs so popular, and what effect are they having on our children?

In trying to answer those questions, I have come to realize that youth sports programs in America are in crisis. Although their popularity is booming, the problems they cause for children and families are also increasing. In these pages I have documented many of the problems caused by adult-organized youth sports programs. They include emotional abuse of children; increased risk of serious injury; exploitation of children; an increase in eating disorders among young athletes; burnout; family conflict; violence among parents, coaches, and officials; mistrust and miscommunication in families, schools, and communities; and much unhappiness for many young athletes. I believe that if this crisis is not addressed, the problems will continue to worsen.

This book is not a sugarcoated portrayal of sports for kids, as so many other books on this topic have been. I want to show you the reality, warts and all, of competitive sports for children. There are many positive aspects to involvement in youth sports programs, but there is a dark side as well. I especially want to emphasize that being a youth sports parent is an emotional challenge.

Ask any parent who has spent years on the sidelines encouraging their fledgling athlete and you will discover that being the parent of a youth sports participant is physically and emotionally draining. There are many rewards, including the thrill of seeing a child discover the self-confidence that comes with mastering a tough challenge. But there are also low points, such as the emotional blow of seeing a youngster in tears after getting cut from a team. Many parents are equal to the challenge and give their children skills that help them cope with the problems they face, not only in sports but in all aspects of life. But other parents are ill-prepared for coping with the experience of parenting a child through a competitive sports experience, and they end up in conflict with their child or imposing their own agenda and by so doing blunting the aspirations of the young athlete.

Despite the enormous popularity of youth sports, we give them little serious attention. Other facets of our children's lives, especially education, have become the focus of intense national debate. We spend much time and money debating the pros and cons of various approaches to education, yet we hardly give a thought to the fundamental life lessons that our children are learning every afternoon on playing fields and in gymnasiums all across the land. This book addresses this issue with the respect it deserves. What are our children learning from their youth sports experience? How can parents help shape this learning experience for the best? Are the youth sports leaders in this country living up to the responsibility we have given them? And how are parents coping with the demands of being a soccer mom or a basketball dad?

I've been involved in youth sports virtually all my life. One of the earliest memories I have is the joy I felt at around age five when I finished in third place in a race at our parish picnic—and the disappointment I felt when the man giving out the awards mispronounced my name. My first competitive sports experience was playing junior football at age eight. Our team was terrible. I think we won only one game in two years, but it was a quintessential youth sports experience—despite the repeated losses, our team always enjoyed itself. By age twelve I took up competitive tennis, a game I have enjoyed now for thirty years. Looking back, I can't thank my parents enough for exposing me to such a wonderful sport. By age sixteen I was coaching junior football. The team of happy six-year-olds I inherited was a fantastic bunch to coach. They soaked up everything about the game. A few years later I became an assistant tennis coach.

The satisfaction I received from playing and coaching sports influenced my decision in psychology graduate school to specialize in the area of sports. It was a decision many of my professors had a hard time understanding. They wanted me to be a "serious" researcher, and they couldn't understand my fascination with the sports experience. But I felt then, as I now know, that sports are a very important aspect of life.

Today I specialize in the psychology of sports. I've been lucky to work with Olympic and professional teams, helping some of the best athletes and coaches in the world. But in my private practice I also see many families struggling with the pressures related to a child playing high-level competitive sports. Many of my clients are young athletes searching to discover their potential in sports. The experiences they have shared with me have led me to write this book. I wanted both to explore the joy these young people get from sports and to try to understand the pain they have suffered as a result of the actions of the adults who were supposed to be looking after them.

Before we tackle this important topic, let me step back and give you a framework with which to view the role of youth sports in our society. I believe that youth sports fulfill two major roles in our culture. First, they promote the development of talent in sports. Second, they are a vehicle for promoting lifelong mass participation in sports and physical activity.

PROMOTING TALENT DEVELOPMENT

The massive system of youth sports in America is the vehicle for identifying, developing, and delivering talented athletes to adult sporting organizations, such as the various professional leagues and the Olympic sports. For professional sports to survive, and for American teams to be competitive in events such as the Olympics, there must be a way of identifying the most talented young athletes and training them until they have the skills to compete at the highest level. Only the best will make it to the top. What happens to the rest is not the concern of those who run high-level sports.

But this talent delivery system is in trouble. Many talented youngsters are dropping out of sports entirely at an early age, and many others never begin to play. A problem for collegiate, professional, and Olympic coaches alike is that many of the young adults who reach the elite levels of sports lack the basic technical skills and the emotional maturity necessary to succeed at the top level. If the talent development system in youth sports were a car, it would need a major overhaul.

PROMOTING PARTICIPATION

But the talent development function of youth sports is operating like a finely tuned racing machine compared to the role that youth sports is playing in promoting a lifelong commitment to sports and physical fitness. As a vehicle for sponsoring mass participation in physical activity, youth sports programs are a huge failure.

A brief look at the statistics reveals the extent of the problem. Only a third of American adults lead an active lifestyle. The rest are sedentary, causing society enormous problems with lifestyle diseases such as cardiovascular disease, obesity, and high blood pressure. Somewhere between the Saturday morning at John Q. Yancy Park and adulthood, most young people lose their natural love of sports and physical activity and stop participating. What should be a natural part of adult life, as it is for children, becomes instead a chore and a responsibility—the dreaded "exercise." A basic philosophy of youth sports is to promote mass participation in physical activity. The hope is that by introducing young people to enjoyable physical activities and sports at an early age we will encourage a lifelong commitment to fitness and physical activity. The reality is that fewer adults than ever are physically active and fit.

These two roles are very important in America. At times they overlap. For example, the development of wonderful athletes such as Michael Jordan and Brett Favre is important to sporting-equipment companies, which hire such athletes to market clothes and shoes to the large mass of people participating in recreational sports. But at times the roles clash. For example, a high school provides a football program in order for the school to achieve athletic glory, not to encourage large numbers of students to play football. A youngster who loves football and burns with a desire to play the game may nevertheless not get a chance if he doesn't have the talent to make the varsity team. Many young people who would like to play sports are shut out of the existing system.

That youth sports programs are failing in both roles, in developing talent and encouraging mass participation, represents a crisis for America. If as a country we are serious about issues such as health, fitness, and the pursuit of excellence, something must be done. We need to change our youth sports programs to align them with our goals and values.

I have found that this crisis has a very human face. In the next chapter I describe some of the situations I have encountered in which our organized sports programs for children have failed both children and adults. These widespread problems are a symptom of the trouble in which we find ourselves. But I have also found that there are many wonderful coaches, parents, and administrators who not only have similar concerns but also have done something to make a difference. I believe that if we share our concerns, share solutions, and face up to the problem, we can tackle it and solve it. My hope in writing this book has been to spur this process forward. Too many of my clients think that their problems are unique, or that there is something wrong with them. There isn't. There is something wrong with youth sports today, and we owe it to our children to change things for the better.

1

THE CRISIS IN YOUTH SPORTS

 My own interactions with the world of youth sports have been many: as a participant, as a coach, as an observer, as a counselor, and now as a parent. My earliest experiences in the world of youth sports were mostly positive. But over the years I have seen increasing evidence of a dark side to youth sports. Burned-out teenage athletes, exploited athletes, troubled families, young athletes with eating disorders, coach-parent conflicts, abusive parents—all are indicators of a deep and continuing problem in youth sports. And as youth sports programs have increased in popularity, the problems seem only to have worsened and become endemic. The longer I spend in the field as a sport psychologist, the more I learn about the potential harm that can be created by participation in youth sports. I believe that we are facing a crisis for our children, and for ourselves. It is time to stop hiding behind the cliché that sports for children are wonderful character builders, and time to find a way to reduce the problems. We must find out how to organize sports programs for young people that are safe and healthy, and that provide positive learning experiences.

My goal is not to demonize youth sports but to examine them clearly, without looking through the distorted attitude of fervent support that we often assume as soon as the topic arises. It is also my hope that we can learn enough about sports, competition, our children, and ourselves to create a uniformly positive sports environment that fosters the growth and development of children and adults. To do that, we must look at the role of sports in the lives of our children, in our families, and in our society and identify the processes that create the problems.

THE DARK SIDE OF YOUTH SPORTS

There is a strong tendency in our society to view participation in sports in a most favorable light. Children are encouraged to participate in organized youth sports programs because these programs are thought to promote such fundamental values as character, teamwork, determination, and commitment. I frequently work in corporate settings and I find that the unquestioning endorsement of the value of the sports experience runs deeply in corporate America. Indeed, the traits valued in corporate settings are often the same as those sought by coaches—leadership, teamwork, and dedication.

This bias toward regarding sports involvement in a positive manner can be troublesome if it blinds us to recognizing that problems exist. In recent years we have come to realize that some professional-level athletes have serious problems—drug and alcohol abuse, spousal violence, and acts of sexual aggression. We now know that the lives of professional athletes are not always happy ones, even when athletes are blessed with incredible talent and large financial rewards. But we have been much slower to recognize the problems inherent in the world of youth sports. Perhaps this is partly because we are much more likely to pay attention to the problems of famous celebrities than to the problems of children. Or perhaps it is partly because we want to believe that youth sports programs are always a positive experience for our children. It is disturbing to look behind the facade and to realize that children participating in organized sport programs are sometimes unhappy, often pressured, and sometimes cruelly exploited. Following are some of the most common problems seen in the world of youth sports.

The Out-of-Control Parent

The young soccer player I observed crying as his father berated him is the visible face of the problem of the out-of-control parent. In their advertising campaigns, big companies love to associate children's sports with ever-smiling, happy faces, but every parent who has been on the sidelines has seen the examples of emotional abuse that are too common in the world of youth sports: the mortified child whose mother is screaming at a referee about a "blown call," the embarrassed child whose father is yelling at the coach about "getting my kid into the game," and the despondent child who is being verbally lashed, again, for some perceived lack of effort or for making a "dumb mistake."

It has become fashionable to blame "pushy parents" for many of the excesses seen in children's sports. I think that this is a mistake. Apologists for youth sports argue that these people are just bad parents who probably often act in an emotionally abusive manner toward their child. I don't think so. I think that youth sports programs bring out the worst in many parents.

Time and time again I have seen well-meaning parents begin to act very much out-of-character as they get caught up in the emotional roller coaster of their child's competitive situation. I believe that this is due to the seductiveness of the youth sports experience, the way it draws those involved into a tangle of emotions. There is a great deal of narcissistic appeal in sports competition, and parents are very susceptible to this when their own children are involved in the competition.

I call this power the dark side of youth sports involvement—the very seductive appeal of sports as an ego trip. Parents who fall into this trap begin to act impulsively, letting their emotions get the better of them, and are often viewed by others as acting like children rather than as adults. You can see examples at many children's sports events. You can see it in the actions of the father, a well-respected businessman, who gets so upset at the calls of the umpire in his son's baseball game that he begins to scream insults at the umpire. I have been at junior hockey games where the game was called off because parents began to fight in the stands. And from many clients I have heard stories of parents of the opposing team shouting abuse and insults at my clients during a game. Frank*, now a college baseball player, recalls a coach stopping a game and pulling him and his twelve-year-old teammates off the basketball court during the league's championship game because of the level of invective coming from the parents of the opposing team.

Supporters of sports for kids dismiss the negative situations as aberrations. Clearly these negative parents have something wrong with them. Good parents never act like that. I believe that adopting this point of view misses the reality of the impact that children's sports has on parents. It isn't that bad parents make the sports experience a bad one. It is that the strong emotions aroused by seeing your own child, your flesh and blood, locked in a competitive struggle with others lure many parents into acting in ways that end up hurting their children, or their relationship with their children. Parents who lack the skills to cope with the powerful emotions of ego gratification triggered in them by watching their child compete are those most strongly affected by participation in youth sports programs. These are the individuals who come to be viewed by others as out of control but who believe they are doing what is best for their child. The question is often asked, Is competition bad for children? We should also ask, Is being the parent of a competitive youth sports participant bad for parents?

Exploitation of Children

For more than seven years I was the resident psychologist at the Olympic Training Center in Colorado Springs. While there I noticed an evolving trend toward children being younger and younger

*Throughout the book I have included many incidents related to me by my clients. In all such cases, I have substantially changed important details, sometimes combining cases, and have not used real names. I do this to preserve the confidentiality of my clients.

when they began to specialize in their Olympic sport. This trend disturbed me, because the commitment level required to become an Olympic athlete is extraordinarily high. There may have been a time when athletes could afford to be "part-time" about their Olympic commitment, but no more. To make an Olympic team, athletes today must commit to full-time training at the highest level for many years. They may be able to juggle school or work around their training, but the training comes first.

This makes me uneasy, because young athletes must make difficult decisions about their level of commitment and dedication to a sport at younger and younger ages. Consider for a moment that researchers have found that it takes about ten years of dedicated practice for an athlete to become an expert in his or her sport. Now consider that at the most recent Olympic Games there were many gymnasts in the women's artistic gymnastics competition who were age fifteen or even younger. By simple arithmetic it's easy to figure out at what age these Olympic gymnasts are beginning to train in order to gain the necessary experience to become world-class by age fifteen.

Those responsible for the high-level sports programs in our country are well aware of the need for children to begin training at a young age if they are to achieve international success. And it is not just gymnastics officials who are concerned about the training of children. For example, when Alan Rothenberg, the president of U.S. Soccer, recently announced a Nike-sponsored program to help identify and recruit talented youngsters into soccer, he commented, "The average age of a World Cup winning player is twenty-eight, which means that we have to be dealing with nine-to-sixteen-year-olds right now."

My worry is over how the decisions are made for such young athletes to begin training at such high intensity. I think that most people would agree that seven-year-olds are too young to make such decisions. Even ten-year-olds may be too young, yet by this age many gymnasts, for example, are already training at a high level.

The parents I know who are in these situations tell me that they are "doing it for my child." But how do they know whether this is indeed the right decision for their child? In sports such as figure skating and gymnastics, I know of many families who actually live apart in order to give their young ten- or thirteen-year-old athlete a chance to train with top-level coaches. Perhaps mother and daughter move to Colorado Springs to train while dad and the other children stay in Detroit. Is it really possible for parents to make such grave decisions "for their children," or is part of the decision based on their own desires and on their own competitive drive?

Reporter Joan Ryan spent several years investigating the training of elite gymnasts and figure skaters, and her conclusion was that the "national appetite for new stars is insatiable. Deep down, we know that our consumption and disposal of these young athletes are tantamount to child exploitation and, in too many cases, child abuse. But we rarely ask what becomes of them when they disappear from view."

These are strong words, but an increasing number of experts agree. In 1993, sociologist Peter Donnelly called for the enactment of some form of child-labor laws that can be used to protect the welfare of elite young athletes. He makes a good point that when parents, agents, and administrators stand to make a large profit from the performance of a child athlete, the young athlete deserves some protection. Are decisions about the child being made for their own good, or can financial incentives cloud the judgment of the adults involved?

Child exploitation in youth sports is not limited to such high-profile sports as figure skating and gymnastics. The potential for exploitation is high whenever youngsters become involved in high-intensity training programs. It is difficult for many thirteen-year-olds to remain committed to a demanding training program, whether the sport be gymnastics, football, swimming, or wrestling, but it is more likely when a determined parent insists that the child continue or risk being a "quitter." Is a child really the one making the decision to commit, or is it the parent's decision? And is the parent standing firm in order to help the child grow in maturity and wisdom, or is the parent influenced by prospects of success and recognition? These are tough questions for concerned parents, and they will be examined in depth in these pages.

No sport is immune from the risks of exploitation. It is present whenever a family faces decisions about how to help a talented child progress to the next level. Indeed, in this day and age I sometimes feel that having athletic talent is a curse rather than a blessing. So much is expected of so-called talented athletes, and often, at the end of the road, after all the struggles, they receive so little for their efforts. The following account of a very troubling situation I encountered several years ago illustrates the dangers of child exploitation inherent in youth sports involvement.

Ken and Bobby

I first met Ken in the sunny waiting area of my office in Connecticut. Tall with blonde hair, very good looking and tanned, Ken looked like a movie star or professional athlete. In fact, he had spent much of his life preparing for a career as the latter. He was accompanied on that first visit by his fiancé, Lisa, and together we walked back to my office.

Ken was twenty-three when he first came to visit. Over the course of the next few meetings, Ken and I began to form the tenuous bond of trust that constitutes the heart of all counseling relationships. Gradually he told me about his life as an athlete. I thought I had heard everything in the world of sports, but Ken's story shocked even me.

The central figure in Ken's saga was his father, Bobby, a big, strong-willed man who had struggled all his life to make a good living for his wife, Marie, and his kids, Sarah and Ken. Bobby was in the business of home repair, and he seemed to be able to do a little bit of everything—plumbing, electrical work, carpentry—whatever the customer needed. As his son grew up, Bobby saw that Ken was a natural athlete. Ken was the biggest in his class, the fastest, and he loved sports—especially those in which he had a chance to use his size and speed to his advantage. Ken's special love was football, and Bobby encouraged his interest by coaching his youngster in the fundamentals of the game. Ken told me of many happy boyhood hours spent playing football outside with his father, throwing and catching and tackling each other until Ken's mother would insist on them coming inside for dinner.

But as Ken grew older, a dark side to Bobby's interest emerged. By the time Ken was twelve, his father had dropped all his other interests in life to focus on Ken's football "career," as he called it. Bobby had been involved in an auto accident, and a large settlement for severe whiplash had left him with some financial security. No longer did he have to neglect Bobby's development as a football player because of work. Now, as soon as Ken came home from school, it was down to the nearby field to work on running and blocking and tackling. Bobby attended every practice and every game of Ken's youth team and began scouting the surrounding high schools to see which one might best advance Ken's career.

It was around this time that Ken remembers being introduced to the "multiformula vitamins" that his father insisted he take regularly. Ken remembers that even as a thirteen-year-old he felt there was something wrong about the secrecy surrounding these vitamins, but it wasn't until he was much older that Ken realized that his father had been giving him steroids. At the same time, Bobby started Ken on a rigorous strength-training program, and the garage of their suburban Texas home was transformed into something resembling the local gym, complete with circuit training equipment and free weights. Ken became bigger, stronger, and better.

The next year, Ken began attending high school on the other side of town. It wasn't the school he had expected to go to, and Ken doesn't know how his father arranged for him to go there, but it had a terrific football team and a well-connected coach. The same year, Bobby was given a part-time job as assistant football coach at the high school. As far as Ken can remember, most of Bobby's duties seemed to center on supervising Ken's training. Ken's memories of these years are not as happy as his earlier memories. Increasingly he viewed his father's attentions as overly restrictive. No matter how well Ken played on Friday evenings, his father was never satisfied. And Ken was able to develop few interests outside school and football. There was just never enough time for them.

Ken's school lost only two games in his freshman season, and Ken was named the All-Conference Freshman of the Year. During the off-season his father arranged for him to have arthroscopic surgery on his left knee to repair some torn cartilage. In the next regular season the team was undefeated and went to the state final, where they lost after Ken hurt his knee badly and had to sit out the second half. The reconstructive surgery on the knee was more extensive this time around and caused Ken to miss the start of his junior football season. When he came back he seemed to have lost none of his dazzling speed, and the team advanced once more to the state final, where they emerged victorious. During his final high school season, Ken and his father concentrated on Ken's establishing the state record for all-purpose yards in a single season, which he did with a game to spare in the regular season. But in his next game, Ken was hit in the back of the knee on a kickoff return and again tore his knee severely.

Naturally Ken had been vigorously recruited by many colleges to join their football programs. Ken remembers going out to his mailbox after school and finding it stuffed with bright, multicolored flyers from schools all over the nation. His father spent hours in his home office poring over the information from the various schools and weighing the pros and cons of each. It turned out that this would be a real family decision. When Ken left Texas to attend college, his family moved with him! The house in Texas was sold, and the family moved to the college town in the southeastern United States that would be Ken's home for the next four years.

It was around this time that the rumors of his steroid use began to circulate. Ken remembers his father becoming enraged by a story he heard about the head coach from one of the other schools that had recruited Ken. This coach had disparaged Ken to some other coaches, calling him a "steroid-enhanced freak." Bobby threatened a lawsuit and a letter of apology was sent, but the rumors didn't stop. In fact, at this time Ken began to suspect that the rumors were true. His father asked him to change from the capsule "vitamins" to some vitamin injections—Ken was now using injectable water-soluble steroids. But Ken was now convinced that the "vitamins" were vital in his efforts to be a great athlete.

Ken's college experience was unusual. His overly supportive family led to him being estranged from his classmates. He formed few friendships, and those few were all with football teammates. Ken was academically talented and did well at school, but football remained the focus of the household. Mom worked a variety of jobs to bring in extra money for the family, Ken's sister Sarah attended a nearby school to study nursing, and Bobby continued to mastermind Ken's career. By now the ultimate goal was clear: Bobby intended his son to have a glowing college career and for him to be a high draft pick in the NFL. Nothing was allowed to interfere with this objective. Even Ken's female relationships were the object of intense scrutiny by his parents, and most of his girlfriends were quickly put off by dating Ken *and* his mother and father.

Despite Bobby's best efforts to orchestrate a perfect script for his son's football career, flaws began to emerge. Ken had two more serious injuries during his time in college. These limited his playing time, and he never became a regular starter on the team. In his final season he was tackled by two burly defenders simultaneously and hurt his back, an injury that was exacerbated at a subsequent weight-training session. As time went on, it became clear that there was little interest in Ken as an NFL prospect. Bobby became quietly desperate, writing to teams and agents trying to generate interest in his son. He had no success. After Ken's final college season, his father tried to sue the college for "poor management" of Ken's back injury, but the suit went nowhere. The family packed their bags and returned to Texas.

For a while Ken lived the life of a beach bum as he tried to come to grips with the loss of his football dream. He met a young college student, Lisa, and moved in with her, a decision that appeared to alienate his father. As he and Lisa became closer, he seemed to become more distant from his parents. Lisa urged him to move on with his career and enroll in a graduate degree program in business, but Ken was becoming increasingly angry and moody, perhaps indicative of his sense of loss of his identity as a football star. He tried to talk to his father about the physical and emotional cost of the years spent out on the gridiron, but Bobby always became upset and the conversations broke down in shouting and angry exchanges. This was a very difficult issue for Ken. He felt the depth of his father's love for him, yet he was unable to reconcile this love with the actions of the man who put him on steroids before he was old enough to realize what was happening.

Lisa was accepted into a graduate design course at a college in New York, and the two moved east. When Ken proposed to Lisa, she agreed on the condition that he seek counseling, and that was how they came to my office for our first meeting.

Ken's story indicates that it is not just very successful athletes who run the risk of being exploited. For every athlete in every sport who becomes a success story, there are scores of others who give an equal effort and make equally difficult sacrifices without ever reaching the top. It scares me to think of how many children there may be with fathers (or mothers) like Bobby, yet we never hear about them.

Youth Sports Dropouts

Another problem for youth sports programs is the huge number of children who stop playing after displaying initial interest. For example, in a comprehensive survey of 1,183 athletes aged eleven to eighteen and of parents of 418 athletes aged six to ten, researchers found that 35 percent of the young athletes planned to stop playing the next year. Nearly half the parents reported that their child was not interested in the sport anymore.

| Several analysts have pointed out that young people today have multiple demands on their time, so the decision that a sport is taking too much time, or a decision to use the time for some other activity, is not worrisome. But my concern is that I see too many young people with a great love of sports who are driven away by the manner in which programs are organized. Somehow we take children, who have a natural desire to be active and to play, and we turn them away from sporting activities. Consider the responses from a survey of 5,800 children who had recently stopped playing a sport. Their top five reasons for stopping were

I lost interest.

I was not having fun.

It took too much time.

Coach was a poor teacher.

Too much pressure.

Only one of these reasons supports the notion that young athletes are turning away from sports in large numbers because of conflicting priorities. The other four reasons indict our organized youth sports programs as failures. These programs fail to meet the needs of children. This indictment is further supported by the answers these children gave when asked what changes might get them involved in sports again. Frequent responses included, "If practices were more fun," "If I could play more," and "If coaches understood players better." Our programs must be better organized to maintain the natural motivation of children to participate.

Endangering the Health of Young Athletes

Another indicator of the crisis in youth sports is the high incidence of problems such as eating disorders, injuries, use of performance-enhancing drugs, and alcohol abuse.

Eating Disorders

Researchers have found that in some sports, such as wrestling, gymnastics, figure skating, and diving, the number of athletes with eating disorders is many times the usual rate found in the general population. In one study of 695 male and female college athletes, researchers found that 39 percent of the female athletes met the criteria for bulimia. This suggests a problem of appalling magnitude. In some sports, an unhealthy focus on weight loss seems to have become an institutionalized form of abuse of young athletes.

The research data support my own observations, for I have counseled an alarming number of young athletes who have eating disorders. Often their sports involvement was a contributing factor to the problem. A judge may have given a young girl feedback that she "looked too heavy" on the ice, or a coach might have told a lineman that he "needed to bulk up in the off-season." Such advice, given to young athletes who may have little knowledge of the basis of a sound dietary approach to weight management, can have devastating effects. The longer young athletes remain involved in competitive programs, and the more pressure they experience to win, the greater is the risk of such problems occurring.

The experience of Jenna, one of the young athletes I work with, shows how insidious the process can be:

> Until my junior year in high school I just loved running. But then my participation in track became a nightmare. My coach had all these strange rules, but the thing that really hurt my performance was the God-awful diet he put us on. It made me lose a tremendous amount of weight, and my desire to run.
>
> My coach weighed us before every practice. He kept very accurate records from day one of how much everyone weighed. Going into the preseason I was 120 pounds. The diet consisted of no soda, Kool-Aid, or alcohol—only

water and Gatorade. He told us only one meal a day and to make it low in fat. It had to be a big meal. My meal for the most part would consist of a huge plate of ziti with sauce, bread with no butter, water, and zucchini. I ate this meal religiously most days of the week. By the middle of the season I was down to 100 pounds. But I was so busy that I did not notice these dramatic changes. The weirdest part of the whole thing was that I felt I was doing better than ever. I even felt stronger and healthier.

But my times did not show that. My times for the 100-yard and 200-yard dash increased almost a whole second! As the weeks went by and I got closer to the end of the season, I went from first heat to last heat. This really stressed me out because I couldn't understand why my performance was not up to par. I told myself that I exercised a great deal and I ate only correct foods. But by the last meet, I realized that this season was the worst that I had ever seen myself run.

Track season ended and I saw some of my old friends from high school. They mentioned that I had lost a lot of weight. After about ten of my friends had commented on how I was so skinny, I slowly started to realize that the reason my performance suffered was due to lack of eating and proper nutrients in my body. Also, after the track season ended I had become obsessed with working out. And I couldn't get myself out of the habit of eating one meal a day. I was getting worse, not better. I felt this was my worst nightmare come true. I did some reading and realized that I had developed an eating disorder. I blamed my coach for encouraging me to become anorexic.

Injuries and Overtraining

It is estimated that four million children seek treatment for sports injuries in hospital emergency rooms each year, and twice that number see a primary care physician for treatment. But on the whole, youth sports programs are doing a much better job today of looking out for the safety of children. Of far greater concern is the rise in overuse injuries among young athletes.

Overuse injuries occur because young athletes train too hard. When the stress on the developing young body is too great, breakdowns occur. Several of my clients, for example, had their elbows ruined for pitching by overtraining, or by trying to learn inappropriate "trick" pitches, such as the curveball, when they were young. The stress is simply too great on their ligaments, tendons, and joints. My sports medicine colleagues report a steady increase in the number of overuse injuries they see in their operating rooms. These injuries are all preventable. Overuse injuries occur because adults push young athletes too hard or too far.

Steroid Abuse

During my time at the Olympic Training Center in Colorado Springs, one of the most challenging problems facing the athletes was the widespread abuse of drugs and artificial substances to enhance performance. In some sports in which strength or endurance was a key factor, there was a broad perception that many athletes were doping their way to the top. This was a very discouraging consideration for many athletes. How could an athlete justify staying in a sport if he thought his competitors were cheating via the use of drugs?

Children are not immune to such problems. South African junior athlete Liza de Villiers was fourteen years old when she tested positive for anabolic steroid use in 1995 and was banned from athletics for four years. In a recent survey of 965 students at four Massachusetts middle schools, researchers found that 2.7 percent of the youngsters were using steroids. This means that children as young as ten, in fifth grade, are using anabolic steroids to change their appearance and performance. It is impossible for children at this age to be obtaining such substances without the direction of adults. It is hard to imagine the pressures being placed on children who begin these dangerous practices at such a young age. It suggests to me that the crisis we are facing is worsening, not improving.

Alcohol Abuse

Alcohol abuse also appears to be higher in some athlete populations than in the general population. It is well known that many sports have a long tradition of promoting alcohol consumption on a social basis (such as keg parties), but does this have an effect on actual alcohol use by athletes? Researchers have found that it may. In one study, intercollegiate athletes were found to have the highest rates of binge drinking of any group of students. In another study by my colleague Chris Carr, male high school student-athletes in a middle-class community were found to have higher rates of alcohol use than other students. There were no differences between female athletes and nonathletes.

These serious health problems would be cause for concern even if they affected only older, more committed athletes. But when we see evidence that these problems are filtering down to children in high school and even middle school, we should be deeply concerned. No trophy or medal or national championship is worth destroying the health of even one child.

Sexual Abuse of Young Athletes

One of the worst violations of the trust we place in the youth sports system is when young athletes are sexually abused. Although several recent cases have made headlines, it is hard to know how extensive this problem is. This difficulty is due in part to the shame and secrecy associated with such abuses of power. University of Winnipeg sociologist Sandra Kirby says it is unusual for an athlete to speak up when caught in such a situation. "It's like being a part of a family," Kirby says. "And athletes [are taught] that it's up to the family to solve their own problems. For an athlete to breach that family trust is very difficult."

Canadian ice hockey coach Graham Jones was recently jailed for more than three years for sexually assaulting two junior athletes, due largely to the courageous testimony of one of the athletes, Sheldon Kennedy. The sexual abuse began when Kennedy was only fourteen years old, and he estimates that he was assaulted more than three hundred times during his junior career. Another athlete who has come forward is Fox sports correspondent Diana Nyad, who revealed that she was raped by her swimming coach. Although his career continued to flourish, she ended up emotionally distraught and in therapy.

Coaching young athletes is an important responsibility precisely because coaches are in a position of power in their relationships with children and adolescents. Coaches who abuse their power and have sex with young athletes are a very small minority, but their existence necessitates that parents keep a watchful eye on their children. Some coaches resent parents who stay closely involved with their young athletes, but if parents and coaches work together they can form a powerful combination to help young people develop. Parents who abrogate their responsibilities for their child and allow the young athlete to live with, or be in the care of, a top coach may be making a much more serious mistake than the overinvolved parent.

Violence in Youth Sports

As an extreme example of how bad things can get in youth sports, the story of high school student Mike Cito and his father Stephen is difficult to beat. According to newspaper accounts of the incident, referees stopped a high school football game when they found that five players had been gashed during the game. They discovered Mike Cito's helmet contained a buckle that had been sharpened like a razor, causing the injuries to his opponents. One player had a wound that required twelve stitches. Mike, a junior, was kicked off his team and expelled from his school, and his father, a dentist, stepped forward and admitted that he had sharpened the buckle because he was unhappy about the unfair treatment his son had received from referees in the previous week's game. What is going on when a father turns his son into a dangerous weapon because he is upset by a referee's decisions?

A recent court case in Connecticut illustrated another type of violence that should have no place in youth sports. A local coach was brought to trial for staying behind after a youth baseball game had finished and physically harassing the umpire, who the coach felt had been unfair in his decisions. The umpire, a volunteer, of course, trying to help children enjoy a game, was sixteen years old.

A friend of mine, known to all as a very gentle and kind person, has been officiating high school and college basketball games for nineteen years, just for the love of the game. But his love of the game was severely tested after one game when a woman, a volunteer assistant coach whose younger sister was in the game, approached him after the game and verbally abused him for some time. When he tried to leave, she attacked him, jumping on his back and hitting him. The reason? She was upset because she did not agree with some calls he had made!

Apologists for this sort of behavior point out that professional sports on television are often violent, such as some of the big hits we see in hockey and football. But this argument really has nothing to do with the violence associated with youth sports. The parents just mentioned are not imitating the pro athletes they see on television—that violence takes place within the game. What is disturbing about the violent behavior we see on the sidelines and in the stands is that it takes place outside the game. Once again, these parents are out of control, behaving in blind response to feelings of anger and frustration generated by watching youth sports. But we should be careful not to exonerate the game too quickly. We need to understand why being involved in youth sports, even as a spectator, has such powerful emotional effects on some parents.

A SEARCH FOR SOLUTIONS
TO THE YOUTH SPORTS CRISIS

The search for solutions to the problems described in this chapter has proceeded apace, but in a piecemeal fashion. Each problem has tended to be treated separately. But what if all of these problems have a root cause? Despite their seeming differences, what if violence in sport, eating disorders, and exploitation of children all spring from the same basic issue?

The cause of the crisis in youth sports, and of all the problems we see in youth sports, is the focus of this book. We need to understand

- The role of youth sports programs in our society and why they are so popular

- The motivations of the parents who participate

- The motivations of the children who participate

- Why parents can sometimes act in such strange and seemingly hurtful ways toward young athletes

- How families can support and help young athletes

- The nature of competition, and the attitudes we develop toward it

- The effects of organized competitive sports programs on children and families

Through an analysis of these issues, I hope to uncover the basic reasons for the problems in youth sports, and from there to move toward solutions to the crisis.

Despite all of the problems, I still believe that youth sports programs can do a great deal of good for children and for families. In the pages ahead I document many of the positive aspects of organized sports for children. But if we are to improve the programs we offer to our children, we need to acknowledge and confront the problems. Not only do we need to understand that youth sports are not just "games for kids," but we also need to understand the important roles they play in our society and the powerful psychological pressures they exert on children, families, and communities.

This book takes a close look at a social process—youth sports—that claims to exist to meet the needs of children but that may be doing more harm than good. A lot is at stake. We cannot let the current youth sports system go lumbering on as it is, for too many families are paying the price of our neglect of the needs of children. A central argument of the book is that youth sports programs do not exist just for children. Parents and other adults are the ones who organize these programs, run them and coach the children, and show up to watch. Youth sports programs are for adults as much as for children—perhaps more so. Until we recognize this fact, we will not be able to organize programs that meet the needs of these involved adults and are also beneficial to children.

This book was written to try to help all parents who enjoy sports and want to provide the best opportunities—safe and happy opportunities—for their children to participate in organized youth sports programs. I hope that we—the adults—can recognize that by placing our needs ahead of those of our children, we are doing them harm and a great disservice. We need to recognize the needs of the adults involved, but we need to organize our programs to best meet the children's needs. I believe we can do it.

I hope you will join me on this journey of exploration into the lives of children and parents involved in youth sports. This will primarily be a journey of the heart. Looking at youth sports will tell us much about ourselves, about the society we live in, and about our attitudes to competition, success, and failure. It's a journey well worth taking, for our own sakes, as well as for our children's.

2

HOW DID WE END UP
IN THIS PREDICAMENT?

The Development of Youth Sports in America

We tend to think of the debate over the appropriate place of children's sports in our society as a recent hot issue, but sixty years ago professionals were engaged in intense debate over these same questions.

Imagine a gathering of teachers, physical educators, and medical and child development experts in the year 1938. World War II is still three years away from dragging the United States into global conflagration, and these esteemed experts have gathered in Atlanta to discuss a more pressing issue: What role should competitive sports play in the lives of school children?

A variety of speakers lend their opinions on the subject. Physicians point out the fragile nature of young bones and the dangers of intense stress on the development of young bodies. Psychologists present research on the mental stress that can accompany competition, even at this young age, and warn against the emotional consequences of overly competitive play. Child development experts caution that the rapidly changing needs of young children are still not understood, and voice their concerns that encouraging a competitive attitude in elementary-age children might not be good for their long-term development. After several days of debate and discussion, the gathering of professionals reaches a consensus. It is clear that organized competitive sports for young children involves an unacceptable degree of risk for the participants. The convention passes a resolution advising school personnel not to organize competitive sports programs for grade-school-age children. Part of the resolution reads: "Inasmuch as pupils below tenth grade are in the midst of the period of rapid growth . . . be it therefore resolved that the leaders in the field of physical and health education should do all in their power to discourage interscholastic competition at this age level, because of its strenuous nature."

The questions raised in Georgia in 1938 are relevant today. Can youth sports be too stressful for some children? Are young bodies overtaxed by competitive sports? And I would add the question, Are parents prepared for the emotional roller coaster that youth sports participation can entail? The rise of youth sports programs was not due to answers being found for these questions. Instead, such issues were shoved into the background as many other groups stepped in to fill the vacuum created by the withdrawal of school support for competitive interscholastic programs for elementary-age children.

THE RISE OF YOUTH SPORTS PROGRAMS IN THE UNITED STATES

By the beginning of the twentieth century, organized sports programs for children, conducted by adults, were becoming increasingly common. One of the major reasons for this development was the combination of industrialization and urbanization. Large numbers of children were grouped together in close proximity, and parents working at factories and mills were unable to supervise their children's play experiences. Organizations such as the Young Men's Christian Association (YMCA) provided many organized sporting experiences for young boys. This was a new development, for until then it was largely unknown for adults to become involved in the play experiences of children.

Other groups, such as the Playground Association of America, soon followed in the footsteps of the YMCA. At first, most of these programs focused on promoting "wholesome" values such as co-operation, discipline, and character development. By the 1920s and 1930s, however, an increasing number of competitive sports programs for children had been established. These programs more openly emulated the professional sports leagues that were rapidly growing in popularity at the same time. Pop Warner football began in 1930 and the famous Little League Baseball was initiated in 1939. Over the years, every major sport at the adult level came to have its childhood counterpart, including Pee Wee Hockey, Biddy Basketball, and junior tennis and ski programs.

In the years after World War II, a rapid rise in the number of children (the so-called baby boom) was accompanied by increasing levels of parental involvement in children's sports. Dads became coaches, officials, and administrators in the burgeoning youth leagues, and Moms became car pool and transportation organizers. Youth sports programs became extraordinarily popular, and a staple of the American way of life, an accepted way for families to have fun with their children—or, I should say, with their sons, for youth leagues for girls were still largely unknown in the 1950s and 1960s, and athletic girls tended to be steered into "feminine" sports such as gymnastics, skating, and diving.

The situation for girls began to change in the 1970s and 1980s as young girls demanded an opportunity to participate in "masculine" sports such as basketball and soccer, and involved parents began to provide increasing opportunities for girls in their sports programs. This change was undoubtedly hastened, especially at the school sports level, by the passage in Congress in 1972 of Title IX of the Educational Amendments Act, which prohibited gender-based discrimination in educational settings that receive federal monies. The huge increase in girls playing in organized and school-based sports programs has been the most significant feature of the youth sports scene in the past two decades.

Today it is estimated that between twenty and thirty million children participate in organized nonschool sports programs, and perhaps ten million children compete in interscholastic sports. The level of involvement can be intense. On average, during an eighteen-week season a youngster spends eleven hours a week participating in his or her sport. Participation peaks at about age twelve and declines thereafter. Youth sports events such as the Little League World Series are shown to national television audiences.

Over the years, participation in organized sports programs for children has grown, the intensity of the programs has increased, and the amount of involvement by parents in such programs has blossomed. What is responsible for this astonishing growth in the youth sports experience?

THE GROWTH OF GLOBAL SPORTS CULTURE

The growth in youth sports has mirrored the boom in professional sports in our society. Indeed, as we stand on the threshold of a new century, an outside observer of American culture would have to say that we are sports-obsessed. Sports programming saturates our televisions, and sports marketing is omnipresent.

Make no mistake that sports have become very big business in the United States—*very* big business. In 1995, it was estimated that the sports industry generated $85 billion worth of business in this country. It is estimated that by 2000 the sporting industry will be worth more than $120 billion, making it one of the top ten industries in the United States. Globally, the growth of the sports machine promises to be even more staggering. Global sports advertising alone is expected to top $25 billion by 2000.

The same adults who are responsible for the rapid growth of youth sports have fueled the growth of this sports culture, both as fans and as participants. For although only a third of American adults lead a physically active lifestyle, that third has turned to a wide variety of sporting interests. Old standbys such as tennis and running have been joined by booms in such sports as skiing and golf, and by many new sports such as mountain biking and triathlon.

Many of these sports have seen dramatic increases in the number of female participants. In addition, sports fans have fueled the growth of professional sports. *Expansion* has been the keyword in baseball, football, and hockey, and well-established male professional leagues have been joined by women's leagues such as the Women's National Basketball Association (WNBA) and the American Basketball League (ABL). Some urban areas have as many as nine or ten professional sport franchises.

Driving the growth spurt in professional sports, of course, has been the media, especially television. The advent of cable television has seen the birth of round-the-clock sports broadcasting, and there now exist several twenty-four-hour sports cable channels. There are all-day sports radio stations, where the participation of fans as call-in commentators is an integral part of the entertainment package, and every newspaper in the country has a section devoted entirely to sports.

Sports are a pervasive part of our culture, perhaps an inescapable experience in modern society. Even in corporate America, the sports lingo of *competition, teamwork,* and *winning the game* is everywhere. It is impossible to imagine growing up in late twentieth-century America without being affected by sports in some way.

Why have sports become so important? To understand the psychological hold that sports exert on us goes a long way toward explaining why youth sports have become such an emotional issue for families. Sports have become big business because so many adults are powerfully attracted to watching sports. Understanding this attraction holds the key to understanding the impact of watching one's own child participate in such a socially significant activity.

THE DRAMA AND MEANING OF SPORTS

Part of the reason that people are attracted to watching sports is the same reason that people are attracted to watching soap operas on television: it's about real life. It has drama and significance. Critics of sport decry it for being "meaningless," but they miss the important point that for the athlete involved the contest is extremely meaningful. A Super Bowl can define a career, or a big tournament win can push an underdog athlete from obscurity into lifelong financial security. People become very involved in watching the story of a star athlete unfold, especially when they feel some bond or connection with the athlete. Witness the tremendous outpouring of media attention and fan sympathy for elite gymnast Kerri Strug when she struggled gamely on an injured ankle to complete her last vault for the USA gold medal–winning gymnastics team at the 1996 Olympic Games in Atlanta. People understood how much the Olympics meant to her and how desperately she wanted to win a gold medal. The fans understood her drive and ambition even as they flinched to see her suffer.

Sports broadcasters understand how important this story line is to the presentation of the sporting event. Watch a televised professional football game and you will see short profiles of the athletes involved sprinkled throughout the program. During the Olympics, when many of the athletes involved are unknown to American audiences, time and care are taken by the broadcasters to develop background reports on the top medal prospects so that viewers may be told the story of the athlete's life. The more meaningful the contest is to the athlete, the more people tend to watch.

Sport sociologist Jay Coakley points out that the drama of a sporting contest depends in part on how it is perceived by the audience watching at home. When the sport is initially marketed to fans of that sport, its appeal depends largely on the *aesthetics* of the sport. Football fans, for example, appreciate the technical skill of the players; their grace as they run, block, and catch; and the commitment to football exhibited by the players. But for a sport to appeal to a wider audience than just football fans–for it to have mass appeal— Coakley argues, the sport must have *heroic* aspects. That is, there is an increasing emphasis on the danger and excitement of the hard hits, on the willingness of players to go beyond their limits to overcome pain and injuries, and on a player's commitment to winning at all costs. Thus sport becomes mass entertainment.

I might add that the distinction between a sport's aesthetic appeal and its heroic appeal mirrors another important theme of youth sports—the distinction between the *participation ethos* and the *spectator ethos*. One of the best things about youth sports are that they are participatory—children who play are actively involved. Yet even by the time children are nine or ten, there is a push toward the selection of the "best" athletes, who get the chance to keep playing, while the "not so good" athletes are discouraged from playing or encouraged to watch the good athletes. This tendency becomes stronger as children get older. By high school it becomes institutionalized, and by college it is an unstoppable force. As adults we naturally tend to be spectators of sports—we watch the professionals play. Despite years of urgings by experts to get fit by being active, the majority of us refuse to become participants in sports or other physical activity.

Group Identity

This is a significant aspect of the support for professional sports teams. Fans gain pleasure from being identified with "their" team—usually the team where they live or where they grew up. Social psychologists have done an immense amount of research into the powerful attraction of belonging to a group. We know that people derive a large part of their identity from belonging to various groups, such as national, ethnic, and work-related groups. As some traditional group associations, such as organized religions and local community groups, have lost their widespread membership, affiliation with a sports team has come to offer a way to belong.

Many of the families I work with tell me how much they value being able to share the experience of sports with their children. Typical is Gina, a single working mother with three children under age ten. "My father loved baseball, and he loved to share his passion with my sister and I. He would listen to games on the radio in the evening, and I would sometimes sit with him and he would explain what was going on. He was always so happy when we talked baseball. I will always remember the first game we went to together in Boston. My sister and I anticipated it for weeks, and our first sight of the Green Monster in Fenway Park was a huge thrill."

Gina enjoys passing on her father's appreciation for baseball to her children. It seems to be a way of strengthening family bonds and of furthering a tradition of participating in something that goes beyond the family. Somehow baseball offers a chance to connect with a community—a community of true fans and baseball lovers. "I can't tell you how I felt when Dad went with my son and daughter to their first game at Fenway. They did the same things I did when I was a child—ate hotdogs, rode the train, did the seventh-inning stretch. And my son went one better than me. He actually caught a foul ball. He slept with that ball for weeks, he was so proud of it. Now that Dad is gone, baseball is one of those things that brings back the warmest memories of him. I always enjoy it, even when the owners and players try to destroy the game."

Children enjoy this aspect of organized youth sport, and their delight in receiving team uniforms and adopting team names is evidence of this. Parents form an interlocking circle of support—organizing travel, arranging fundraisers for the team, sharing war stories of past triumphs and defeats. Parents identify with their daughter's team, or with their son's skating club. The strength of this identification process should not be underestimated. In an age where other group identities are diminishing, sporting allegiances are gaining strength. National and sporting allegiances mesh at international events such as the Olympics. And although the stakes are not high in the youth sports experience, the identification is stronger when your own flesh and blood are involved.

The Role of Youth Sports

Recognizing the drama and meaning of sports and the role played by the sense of belonging to a group helps us understand why sports have come to play such a central role in American culture, and why youth sports have come to have such emotional significance for American families.

Why have organized sports programs for children become so extraordinarily popular? There is no simple answer, and the complex answer involves understanding our society and culture as much as it involves understanding our individual psychology. The decision to involve a young child in a sports program is largely made by the parents, although the child has more say in the matter as she grows older. But once the decision is made, it involves the whole family, and parent and child become locked in a complex dance of action and reaction, cause and effect, as the child's involvement has a ripple effect on family relationships and motivations.

To understand why participation in sports can cause the sorts of problems we saw in Chapter One, we need to understand thoroughly these social and psychological pressures.

LOOKING INTO THE FUTURE: WILL YOUTH SPORTS PROGRAMS CONTINUE TO FLOURISH?

The numbers alone tell of the astonishing growth of youth sports programs over the past thirty years. Beyond the numbers, however, there are many other signs of the change that has taken place in children's sports.

Equipment is a good example. When I was a youngster, a solid pair of sports shoes and a jersey was all that was required for participation in most sports. Now parents feel compelled to buy their children the latest sports apparel, including a variety of shoes for specific sports and for cross-training, brand new uniforms for each sport, and high-tech versions of standard equipment such as bats and rackets. A time traveler from thirty years ago would find it hard to recognize the landscape of children's sports that exists today.

I see five factors that will ensure that organized youth sports programs continue to flourish in the years ahead:

1. *Continued growth of the sports culture*. There is no reason to believe that the growth of the sports culture in our society will abate. Indeed, it could be argued that children are increasingly being targeted as sports consumers. Witness the growth of television commercials aimed specifically at children that lionize the star athlete. Footwear companies seem very fond of this type of commercial.

Adults who are fans of professional sports are likely, I believe, to enjoy watching their children play in professional-like sporting events such as Little League. The growth of such leagues for young girls is likely to continue to spur the overall growth of youth sport programs.

2. *Parental need for organized out-of-school programs*. The societal pressures on parents to keep their children involved in organized and supervised programs when out of school will not decrease in the foreseeable future. Looked at in the larger context, our society does not provide parents with many alternatives in the child care area. After-school programs tend to be limited and expensive. Organized youth sports programs will continue to be an attractive option, especially as they promote wholesome American values such as teamwork and discipline.

3. *The growth of female participation in sports*. Because girls were excluded from so many sports for so long, sports programs for girls have been the most rapidly growing programs in the last twenty years. This trend will persist as Title IX continues to have an effect on increasing the opportunities for girls and young women to play sports. Also, the growth of opportunities for women to compete in high-level sports programs, such as in the Olympics and in the WNBA and the ABL, will provide young girls with more and more role models in the years ahead.

It will be interesting to observe how our society, which so often treats men and women differently, will cope with these changes. For example, I have already seen fathers who tolerate strict and negative coaching for their sons be much less tolerant of such coaching for their daughters. These parents are often prime movers in efforts to obtain equality of resources and opportunities for girls in sports programs.

4. *Increasing corporate involvement in youth sports.* The interaction of the business world and the sports world has percolated down to the level of youth sports, as can be seen from all the commercial sponsorships on the uniforms of youth baseball teams. There has always been a natural affinity between business and sports, with their shared jargons of *competition, killer instinct,* and *winning attitude.* Promoting youth sports programs is seen as a very positive way to enhance the image of businesses.

Additionally, the growth in youth sports has led to the growth of the youth sports apparel industry. Companies such as Nike and Reebok spend millions of dollars attempting to get youngsters to identify with their brand, knowing that the payoff is huge. This nexus between sports and corporate America will continue to fuel the growth of children's sports in the years ahead.

5. *Promotion of celebrity sports figures as role models for children.* There has always been a focus on sports celebrities as role models for children. Collecting baseball cards that contain the annotated biographies of the stars of the day, for example, is a hobby that goes back more than fifty years. In today's culture, however, the pairing of sports celebrities with children's interests is omnipresent. Michael Jordan, the most famous athlete on the planet, is paired up with Bugs Bunny and other cartoon characters in the movie *Space Jam,* which was aimed at the eight-to-fifteen-year-old market. Shaquille O'Neal, another hugely popular basketball star, hosts a popular television show on the children's cable network, *Nickelodeon,* that deals with serious sports issues.

Youth sports programs offer children a chance to act out their fantasies and imitate their sporting idols. Surveys indicate that many children are initially attracted into sports such as basketball because of their liking for a particular sports star. Organized children's sports programs will continue to grow because they offer kids a chance to "be like Mike."

Youth sports have flourished during a period when the sports culture has become pervasive in American society. Yet to understand the reasons for the myriad problems we see in youth sport programs today, the individual motivations of those involved must be examined closely. What do parents get out of their participation in youth sports?

3

WHAT DO PARENTS WANT?

Many adults who think back to their own childhood sports involvement and compare it to how children play sports today are amazed. The differences are stark. The whole notion of sports organized by kids themselves has almost disappeared. What happened to sandlot baseball and street stickball? When, exactly, did each youth team get its own corporate sponsor? How can parents afford the time to travel with their children to so many "all-star" competitions, even in other states? When did national rankings of high school teams in various sports begin? And were parents always this vociferous on the sidelines during games?

My sport psychology colleagues have studied these issues mainly by examining the reasons that children play sports. Like most of us, they've bought into the idea that youth sports are primarily for children. Consequently, there is a large body of research, which I discuss in the next chapter, that has examined the reasons that children give for why they play youth sports.

But I happen to think that this research is a case of putting the cart before the horse. Although it is certainly worthwhile to find out what children get out of participation in organized youth sports programs, the real engine driving the growth in sports for children is the *parents*. It is parents who typically make the decision to sign their child up for a youth soccer or baseball program, parents who take their children to practices and travel games, parents who spend lots of money on the latest equipment, and parents who provide support at very expensive regional, national, and international youth sports competitions.

Without the efforts of parents and other adults, youth sports programs as we know them would not exist. We call these programs "organized" for a good reason—they are administered, conducted, officiated, and supported by adults. It is adults, not children, who organize leagues, provide coaching, furnish referees and officials, make facilities and playing fields available, send scores to the newspapers, buy trophies for the kids, keep league standings, and select all-star teams. Yet we know very little about the motivation of parents in this area. Why do parents go to all this trouble for their kids? What do they get out of it?

THE BRIGHT SIDE
OF PARENTAL MOTIVATION

There is little, if any research to help answer the question of *why* parents get involved in youth sports programs in such huge numbers. Soon, I hope, sport psychologists will explore this issue and give us good answers based on sound research. In the meantime, let me offer some reasons I have observed in my years of working with parents and children in sports—factors that motivate parents to choose youth sports programs when making decisions about how to use time with their family. I have also observed several other factors that help explain why parents become so intensely emotional about their involvement in youth sports. I describe these *psychological* factors after I examine the principal motivations of parents involved in youth sports.

Bonding with a Child

Sports has become one of the best and most acceptable ways for parents to spend time with their children. The time pressures that families face today, with the multiple demands of work, home life, schooling, social and community activities, and leisure time, have been well documented. In this environment, spending an hour or two at a child's baseball game or swim meet becomes a valuable way of sustaining a close relationship with the child. Parents often tell me how much they look forward to going to their son's game or daughter's meet. It is a positive experience for the parent.

At a time when many parents worry that they are not spending enough time, or enough "quality" time, with their children, the option of spending time together involved in something fun, such as baseball or soccer, is extremely appealing. Parents take comfort from the fact that their children can enjoy themselves with friends and perhaps learn some valuable life skills, such as concentration and discipline, in the process.

Another attractive aspect of organized youth sports programs is that there are some clear roles for parents. Parents feel that they make a contribution to the team when they organize car pools, keep score, keep the time for the game, find sponsors, help organize the schedule, or help with fundraising. Children's sports programs cannot exist without such parental support.

Perhaps even more fundamentally, many youth sports programs need parents to serve as coaches. Especially at the junior and recreational levels, it is almost part of the deal that parents who sign up their child to play are expected to help out with the coaching as well. Coaching at the junior level is purely voluntary, and youth sports leagues could not survive without the support of many volunteer parent-coaches. Of course, being both a parent and a coach often results in even more challenges for the family.

Providing a Supervised Structure for Free Time

As well as allowing parents to spend time with their child, sports programs help parents structure their child's free time. Some experts, such as my colleague sport sociologist Jay Coakley, have argued that in the past twenty years, parents have been burdened by a new societal expectation—that a "good parent" knows where his or her child is twenty-four hours a day. This expectation did not exist in times past. When I think back to my own childhood, I know there were many afternoons when my mother knew vaguely that I was "somewhere" in the neighborhood with my friends, but she could not have known where we were or exactly what we were doing. Today, parents worry about even basic safety issues when their children are alone, and the thought of children "roaming" a neighborhood unsupervised can be a frightening one. When parents cannot look after their children themselves, they often try to find adult-led programs that ensure constant supervision of children.

Organized youth sports programs provide such an environment. Practices are often held several times a week, offering parents the chance to drop kids off and pick them up a couple of hours later. During this time, parents do not have to worry about where their children are or what they are doing. For many parents, organized youth sports programs are a superior alternative to having their child spend several afternoon hours in front of the TV set.

Excitement and Meaning

I rarely see "adding excitement to life" mentioned in research articles as a reason why families participate in youth sports programs. Yet I have found that this aspect of youth sports is a very real incentive for many.

Ralph, a personnel manager at a large industrial firm, voiced his feelings to me when we were discussing his youngest son, a high school football star. "It was a great time while it lasted," Ralph reminisced. "I never pushed Mike to play football, but he was always a natural at it. He could just throw the ball on a dime from an early age."

Ralph went on: "When he became the starting quarterback in high school, I had never really experienced anything like that before. They made such a fuss about him. He was in the local papers, everyone talked to me about him, and the games. . . ." He trailed off, wistfully. "Friday nights were a big deal. Mike would get so excited and pumped up before games. I couldn't help feeling nervous myself. And there were usually big crowds, and they would be cheering for him, for my son. The team was so successful, and that made Mike feel good, and it made all of us, his Mom and me, feel good."

When Mike graduated, the cheering stopped, and nothing replaced it. "I'm almost ashamed to admit it, but I miss those years," Ralph continued. "There's been nothing to replace all that. Sometimes I feel as if I'm just sort of drifting now. I know Mike's struggling, and that makes it worse. He dropped out of college after one year, and he's hanging out now with a group that just seems to want to party and have fun. It's hard going from being the star to trying to make something of yourself."

Most of the parents I speak to look forward eagerly to their child's weekend games, to trips away with an all-star team, and to the thrill of play-off games. Against the daily grind of stressful jobs and frantic home lives, the excitement and glamour of a child's sporting involvement provide welcome relief. For many families, youth sports involvement offers a rare chance to participate in a community activity. Families come together to support their children's team, and there is a sense of belonging, whether to a school or to a local sports club. Such feelings of involvement and contributing to a group are important to families, and I believe they are a major reason why youth sports programs continue to thrive. It has been fashionable for critics to deride sports as "irrelevant" and "meaningless," but I think the tale told in this book shows that sports are a very meaningful part of life for many people. And there is no need to apologize for that.

Helping a Child's Physical Development and Health

Parents feel good about a son or daughter becoming involved in a sports program because they know that such a program involves physical activity and that it is a sharp contrast to other leisure activities such as watching television or playing video games. Most popular youth sports, such as soccer, gymnastics, swimming, and basketball, involve a lot of vigorous physical activity. Even in sports that are less active, such as baseball, youth coaches usually design practices to involve lots of running and jumping.

Researchers have found that young people who are active in sports programs tend to benefit in a wide range of related areas, including having higher levels of self-confidence, doing better academically, feeling more fit and happy, and even, on average, having fewer problems such as teen pregnancy and dropping out of school. These positive effects of participation in youth sports programs are a good reason to encourage children to play sports, but care must be taken not to ignore the problems described in Chapter One. Youth sports participation can be helpful to many young people—but it can also have very harmful consequences for some. When I contrast the positive effects just described with the problems I documented in the first chapter, I notice that *overinvolvement* in sports may be the biggest problem. Perhaps sports programs give some individuals who might otherwise experience out-of-sports problems (such as teen pregnancy or academic problems) a focused experience that helps them avoid such problems. But for those individuals who succumb to the intense, win-at-all-costs mentality of sports, over-involvement may lead to common sports-related problems such as injury, drug abuse, cheating, and violence.

Also, the popularity of sports for children has done very little to influence the health and activity level of adult Americans. Two-thirds of Americans still live largely sedentary lifestyles, increasing their risk of a range of lifestyle-related diseases. The fact that so many children are such active youth sports participants has not led us to be active and healthy adults.

Teaching a Child Self-Control

A significant attraction of sports programs for some parents is the opportunity such programs offer to teach children self-mastery skills such as discipline and respect. I have found that certain sports actively market this aspect of their program to parents. Some of the martial arts, such as judo and karate, for example, place a heavy emphasis on the responsibility of the child to learn respect and honor for the teacher, or coach. Participants are taught to be respectful of their instructor and of one another, and "fooling around" is not tolerated in most programs. Parents who have a child who has problems paying attention or following directions may be favorably disposed to a sports program that promises to teach the child discipline and self-control.

Most sports programs for children, at least at an implicit level, claim that they teach children certain fundamental values that will be helpful to the child as an adult. Some sociologists argue that this factor has been an important reason for the growth of children's sports in the United State. Sports, they argue, have offered adults a convenient method for preparing children for adulthood, teaching them to be competitive, team players, and achievement oriented.

I think that the fun, fantasy, and excitement offered by youth sports programs are much more important reasons for their popularity, but it is true that every sport has its own "culture," which is passed on to the child through coaching, exposure to professional players, and learning about the history of the game. Football, for example, emphasizes unselfish loyalty to the team, grit and determination, all-out effort, and physical exertion and contact. Sometimes parents worry that the values promoted by a particular sport may *not* be helpful to their child. Many parents, for example, tell me that they worry about the high violence levels in junior ice hockey and how that might encourage their child to be too aggressive.

Developing Talent

Mary brought her son, Jack, to see me because she worried that he wasn't "making the most of himself" in wrestling. Jack made an immediate physical impact when he entered my office. He was tall and strong, with obvious muscle development in every body area, especially the chest and legs. When we shook hands, I worried for the safety of my fingers. Jack had taken up wrestling two summers ago, at age fourteen, and was now highly rated, both in his school and at the state level. Mary had been told several times by his coaches that he was "something special" and they expected great things from him. What Jack expected from wrestling, however, was hard to say. He had an easygoing, relaxed personality, loved joking around, and seemed to take nothing too seriously. When forced to make a choice between social commitments and wrestling, Jack usually chose to be with his friends. This worried his parents, who felt that there was real danger of Jack "wasting his talent."

I have seen similar beliefs expressed by many parents who see in their child some special abilities that might make them especially well-suited for a particular sport. In such a situation, the parent often becomes fixed on the idea of helping the child develop that special talent to the fullest. Problems arise when the motivation of the child to develop that talent is at a different level than that of the parent. Of course, the reverse can also be true. I have had clients who felt very unsupported by their parents, who perhaps did not understand or care as deeply about the sport as their child did.

Promoting Social Development

Finally, some parents look to sports participation as a way of helping their child become more socially adept. Children who have a tough time making friends, or who seem to have problems getting along with other children, might be steered into youth sports that guarantee a variety of social interactions in an adult-supervised setting. Team sports such as baseball, soccer, and basketball are often favorite choices of parents who wish to promote the social development of their son or daughter. My own casual survey of parents indicated that the belief that team sports are "good for kids" because they encourage children "to be more social" is a widely held one.

The factors I have just described are the surface issues, which are only the rational reasons that parents support their children's participation in organized sports. These factors do not explain why the problems we examined in Chapter One occur. To understand the emotional intensity that I see among family members—which observers notice on the sidelines and in the stands of youth sports games, which officials feel as invectives are hurled at them, and which coaches deplore as they struggle to please both parents and administrators—we must dig deeper. There is a psychology of youth sports participation. It is little explored and little understood, but its ramifications have an impact on everyone involved in organized youth sports programs today.

THE DARK SIDE OF PARENTAL MOTIVATION

What is it about youth sports that can arouse such intense passions? Why do we sometimes see fights in the stands between parents of youth sports participants? Why would a mother call a reporter every night for three weeks cajoling him to write something about her son's swimming records? And on a positive note, what keeps families going when the child is a talented athlete and everyone must make financial sacrifices and invest time and energy in the athlete's development? There are deeper motivations behind the involvement of families in youth sports than those already discussed.

The Process of Identification

The first factor we must understand is that parents have a deep and powerful love for their children. The power of this love cannot be underestimated. In my experience, this love leads parents to adopt certain attitudes when it comes to their child's involvement in youth sports:

continued

- *They want the best for their child.* They want their child's sporting experiences to be happy and productive.

- *They want to protect their child from harm.* No parent wants to see their child hurt, emotionally or physically.

- *They hope that their child will excel.* There is a natural tendency to want to see one's own child outperform the other children.

- *They fantasize about what might be.* Parents have many hopes, dreams and expectations for their children, and in youth sports settings these dreams are often played out publicly.

The result of these attitudes is that parents usually become very emotionally involved in the youth sports experience. As a psychologist, I describe this process as *identification*—the parent experiences strong emotions in response to what happens to the child, because the parent identifies so strongly with the child.

If youth sports were just about play, they would not be such an emotional topic. But youth sports involve competition, and this is what makes them intensely involving. We see our children begin to compare themselves to others, and the evaluations are often not favorable. Our children experience failure and loss, and often this is an upsetting experience. Their young desires and hopes are often frustrated by the coldness of reality, and there's not much we can do to change it. Few experiences match youth sports for generating a clash between hopes and reality.

Parents can often smooth out the bumps in other life areas, helping make easier the transition from dependence to independence. Mom can mediate a dispute between siblings about who gets to watch their favorite show, and Dad can help his daughter with a tough homework problem. But there is little a parent can do but watch once the child pulls on a sports uniform and goes out onto the field to compete with others of the same age. Naturally this loss of control can generate a great deal of anxiety for the concerned parent.

There are few life experiences that can generate the anxiety and tension of watching your own son or daughter participate in a sporting contest. There is a strong visceral and emotional connection because of the adult's identification with the child. For the parent, the drama of their child's sporting contest becomes more intense the more it means to the child. A big game becomes a powerful emotional experience for both parent and child. Also, parents know how much effort their child has exerted to reach their current level of skill and competitiveness. The greater the effort that has been expended, the more it means to the parent.

Parents have told me many strange stories about the impact of this anxiety on their behavior at youth sports events. One hockey mother refused to watch the game when her son was playing, retreating underneath the stands to smoke a cigarette whenever his shift took the ice. A gymnastics mother hid in the bathroom, listening for the audience's response as a clue to how her daughter was doing. Several parents I know refuse to go to the games at all, afraid that their nerves will betray them in the heat of battle.

This process of identification helps us understand what happens to youth sports parents as they become more involved in their child's endeavors. It explains the incredible jubilance when a child succeeds, the devastating sense of personal failure when a child's team loses, the way parents can take criticisms of their child so personally, even from a coach. Unfortunately, the strength of the love of a parent for a child, which can be such a great resource to help the child cope with the challenges of becoming a good athlete, can become a handicap when the parent steps over the line and acts irrationally, or irresponsibly, because of the depth of the feelings they have for their child.

The love and support that can be such a strength of many families can in certain situations cause pain and suffering when the parent takes the child's setbacks too personally. Identification with one's child is a natural process. But overidentification can lead a parent to ignore the child's emotions and goals. The overidentified parent mistakes his own feelings and goals for those of the child. Parents who act on their own feelings often end up helping themselves but ignoring, hurting, or frustrating the child.

Dreams of Glory

By the time my son was seven, he knew far more about Michael Jordan and Shaquille O'Neal than he did about Bill Clinton and George Bush. In a society that focuses an enormous amount of media attention on celebrities, sports stars are among the biggest celebrities out there.

There has been a great deal of debate about the extent to which these sports stars are role models for children in our society. Whether the actions of sports celebrities on and off the court noticeably influence the behavior of children is debatable. What is clearly true is that many children, perhaps most, entertain fantasies of living out experiences based on the actions of their sporting favorites. What Little Leaguer hasn't imagined at some time that he is at the plate with the score tied in the bottom of the ninth inning of the deciding seventh game of the World Series? It's a wonderful fantasy, both helping to motivate the child to continue her own sports participation, and adding excitement to her youth league contests. Children naturally identify with their sports idols.

But parents also tend to have similar fantasies about their children. This is particularly true for parents of talented young athletes, who begin to allow themselves fantasies of "what if?" scenarios. What if my son makes the big leagues? What if my daughter plays on the U.S. soccer team? Combine this natural parent-child emotional connection with the elements of heroism present in sports and you begin to see another reason that youth sports participation becomes such an emotional issue. For the child it is natural to see a sporting contest as a chance to play out childhood fantasies of being like Mike, of pretending to be in the Super Bowl or the World

Series. For the parent, the child's sporting competition becomes as personally meaningful as a professional sporting event. The uniforms, the referees, the coverage in the local media, the spectators—all of these combine to mimic what the parent sees when they turn on the television. The youth sports competition becomes a miniature version of big-time sports, with one important addition. One of the athletes involved is the *parent's own child*.

No wonder parents on the sidelines get excited! The fact that youth sports give a parent the chance to see their son or daughter become a hero makes it is easy to see why parents get so frustrated if their hopes and expectations are dashed. Woe to the coach who doesn't give the child a chance to score the winning touchdown or hit the game-breaking home run!

The Young Athlete as an Investment

Another factor that helps to explain the emotional intensity created in parents by youth involvement in sports is the tendency to view the child's athletic success as a just reward for the parent's investment of time and energy. This attitude, all too common in youth sports, is exemplified by one of my clients, Ted, a successful entrepreneur whose daughter was a standout softball pitcher in high school. Ted asked his daughter, Stephanie, to see me to work on her "mental toughness" on the mound, but in counseling sessions with Stephanie she told me that her father's constant pressure on her to succeed was a big reason why she lacked confidence. When I discussed this with Ted, he provided an interesting point of view. His main concern, he explained, was that Stephanie get a full scholarship for softball to a "good school." Ted had never had a college education, though he felt he was smart enough to have done well in school, so one of his main life goals was to see both his daughters attend one of the prestigious private colleges in the northeast.

Ted's eldest daughter had already disappointed him in this goal. An excellent high school swimmer, she had decided to attend a large state school in the Midwest. Consequently, Ted was now totally focused on "helping" Stephanie excel in softball, so she could get a scholarship to one of the schools his other daughter had rejected. Ted's help included extra practice sessions one-on-one with Stephanie, helping out her high school coach as an assistant, and being a vociferous fan in the stands during games.

"All I want," Ted told me, "is for Stephanie to be good enough to deserve a full ride to one of those schools she needs to go to."

Ted's view of Stephanie's participation in softball is an example of how many parents today view youth sports—not as a fun activity for their child, or even as a means to promote good health and fitness, but as a means of achieving a desired goal. The goal can be a college scholarship, a contract with a sponsor, a professional sports career, or a variety of objectives reflecting the achievement of fame, glory, power, or material rewards. Parents today seem especially susceptible to this attitude. Many of my clients have told me that they see money spent on their son's or daughter's sport as an "investment," because they expect some kind of payoff down the road. Instead of enjoying their child's sports experience, these parents spend time worrying about whether progress is being made toward the long-term goal of the investment.

This attitude has spread through youth sports to an alarming extent in the last decade. Parents have begun to see sports not as an end in itself, as something to be enjoyed for its own sake, but as a means to an end, as a vehicle for achieving something else. You can see the effects of this attitude in the mother of a strong young skater, who sits in the stands watching every one of her thirteen-year-old's practices as if she had no outside life of her own. You can see this attitude in the father who has his young daughter out on the golf driving range, pushing her to hit ball after ball, even though her body language shouts loudly that she would rather be doing anything other than swinging this stupid stick around.

I saw the effect of this attitude the other night when I was playing tennis. On the adjacent court, a father was helping his eleven-year-old son improve his game. Together they hit ball after ball, until the court was littered with them, a familiar ritual to young athletes and their coaches everywhere. But every five minutes the boy's mother, who was watching the practice session through a window, would appear in the doorway and scream advice at her husband to hit the balls faster, to give the boy more backhands, and to push him harder. Her loud yells were most unpleasant to hear, and they weren't even directed at me! It seems that a fixed focus on the possible payoffs of the future can easily ruin the enjoyment of the present sports experience.

This attitude not only spoils the enjoyment of sports for a young athlete, it can also lead to the athlete viewing herself as an object. For example, she no longer sees herself as "Stephanie, who loves softball and is good at it," but as "Stephanie the softball player." Her self-image becomes one-dimensional and limited. This problem is especially troublesome for elite athletes, such as the pros, who put considerable time and emotional energy into their sport. But I have seen athletes in their early teens who struggle with a similar self-image.

The effect of seeing sports as just a means to an end can be devastating to youth sports programs. When parents, coaches, and administrators focus on youth sports as a means of achieving their own goals, sports stop being for the kids. When the needs of the children are left out of the equation, sports become a hollow experience indeed.

Competition Between Parents

We have seen that children's competition is emotionally involving for parents because they identify so strongly with their children. Youth sports competitions are emotionally intense because the parent is *sharing* the emotional experience of the child (often experiencing even more competitive anxiety than the child does). But children's sporting competitions also affect parents in another way. Parents sometimes feel competitive with other parents over whose child is the better athlete.

Once again, there is a healthy basis for this competitive attitude. It is natural for parents to feel pride when their child succeeds in sport. But for some parents, feeling good about a child's sporting accomplishments only occurs when the child outperforms other children. These parents need to see their child win the race, score the most goals, or get the most hits in a game. If other children do better than their child, this parent feels jealous and resentful. As I explain in Chapter Seven, there are two basic attitudes toward competition—an ego attitude and a mastery attitude. Parents who have an ego attitude toward their own competition—that is, they compete to win and to be better than others—are especially likely to be competitive with other parents about their child's achievements. We might say that the parent goes from being proud to being boastful.

Of course, parents are competitive about their child's accomplishments in many areas besides sports. It is common to see parents become very competitive about a child's academic progress, which leads parents to pressure children to get good grades and to get into "good" schools. This pressure can take its toll on children who are pushed too far too fast. The tragic case of Jessica Dubroff, the seven-year-old child pilot who died when her plane crashed on takeoff as she attempted to fly across the United States, illustrates the dangers of parents' attempts to guide their children to excel in competitive endeavors by taking risks. It is easy for parents to become very competitive when it comes to youth sports, because the child's accomplishments are so obvious. A "soccer mom" can experience the pride of being congratulated by all the other parents when her nine-year-old child scores a hat-trick in the state tournament. But she can also feel ashamed when her daughter misses a penalty kick in the final game, ending the team's season. I believe it is easy for ego-oriented parents to become competitive with other parents in such situations. The sports environment also encourages the public display of emotion, and this may foster overt expression of competitiveness in some parents.

Parents also get upset if they feel that other children are being given preferential treatment by the coach, at the cost of neglecting their own child. I have found that there is one issue, above all others, that triggers this response in many parents. It is the issue of playing time.

Parents, remember, want to see their child do well in sports, and they want their child to be happy. But parents who feel that their child is not getting an equal chance to play, or who believe that their child is sitting on the bench more than the other children on the team, are likely to feel very frustrated and upset on behalf of the child. The parent's own goals (to see my child play and be happy) are being thwarted, usually by the coach. I have seen this lead to great unhappiness and bitterness. Most parents, and most athletes, too, have the expectation that the youth sport experience will be *fair*, that it will give everyone an equal chance to prove themselves. If a coach is perceived to be unfair, to give some children more chances than others, parents and athletes are likely to become upset. The tension between parents and coaches can become great.

Both parents and coaches today acknowledge the growing rift between them. Coaches tell me that their biggest headaches are caused by parents, and that the most frequent source of contention is the athlete's playing time. Parents, on the other hand, most often complain to me that their child's coach is unfair, plays favorites, or doesn't explain his decisions. Frequently stuck in the middle of these conflicts is the young athlete.

These, then, are the four psychological factors that must be recognized as we try to understand the youth sports experience of families: the identification of the parent with the child, the tendency of parents to fantasize about their child's potential, the sense of youth sport as an investment, and competitiveness between parents. Combined, these factors drive many parents to push their child to excel, and to take action when they feel that their child's potential is being ignored or inhibited.

Now that we have seen why parents want their children involved in organized sports, and why they experience such strong emotions when they do become involved, we can take a look at the reasons that children agree to participate. For although organized youth sports programs could not exist without parents, they thrive only because children find many of their needs satisfied by participating. Some of these needs include the need to please parents, but there are many other sources of motivation for children involved in sports.

4

WHAT DO KIDS WANT?

Sport psychologists have surveyed, questioned, and probed tens of thousands of children to determine why they participate in sports. This research is based partly on the assumption that it is children who decide whether they wish to participate in sports programs. As I have suggested, this is a questionable assumption. Parents have a decisive influence on whether their children participate in sports, especially at a young age, and this influence remains strong as children grow older. Even at the high school and college levels, I have observed subtle power struggles between parents and children over whether and in what form to continue sports participation.

But it is also true that many children, once exposed to youth sports involvement, enjoy the programs. And they find new reasons to sustain their interest as they grow older. It is important to keep in mind that children's needs change dramatically as they age. The reasons that a five-year-old gives for her T-ball participation will be different from the reasons given by a fourteen-year-old for playing freshman baseball in high school. The findings of the researchers who have studied the motivations of young athletes provide a useful starting point for our understanding of the needs of children.

WHY CHILDREN PARTICIPATE
IN YOUTH SPORTS PROGRAMS

One of the first things I noticed about working with young athletes is that there are tremendous differences among them in the ways they approach sports. Some children are very competitive, others not at all so. Some take the rules seriously, others ignore them. For some children, perfecting a new skill is a serious matter, but others never seem to learn the basics. Underlying these great differences are a variety of motives for participating in youth sports. Sport psychologists have identified several basic themes that occur over and over again when young athletes are asked why they play the game.

Fun

"Having fun" is the main reason for playing sports given by children ages five to seventeen. Although pleasure and enjoyment are obviously critical factors in a child's decision to keep playing a sport, *fun* is very difficult to define, and it is difficult to build fun into all youth sports programs.

For example, is it fun to be a runner, to go out on two- and three-mile runs, and to work hard at improving speed over longer and longer distances? Many children I speak to feel that it is. They love running, and it becomes a passion for them. But many other children feel differently. They dislike running. It makes them feel slow and clumsy and tired, and they avoid it whenever possible, even if it is part of training for another sport they enjoy. So is running fun? The answer is, it depends. That's why it is important to understand for each individual child what it is about the sports program they enjoy that makes it fun. All of the following reasons that children give when asked why they like to play organized sports also contribute to making sports fun.

In my work with young athletes, I try to remember a very simple definition of fun and enjoyment that has been provided by University of Chicago psychologist Mihaly Csikszentmihalyi. His theory of *flow* states that people are happiest when the challenge they are facing is equal to the skills they have. This is a great idea to remember when thinking about children in sports. Coaches, administrators, and parents should always strive to provide a challenge to children that is commensurate with their sporting ability. If children are provided with a challenge that is beyond their athletic ability, anxiety is likely to result. If children are skilled and the challenge is not great enough, boredom is the likely outcome. As children develop their athletic skills and confidence, greater challenges must be provided to give them an opportunity to stay in the flow.

Activity and Involvement

It's fun to play; it's boring to sit and watch. This factor is mentioned over and over again by children when I ask what is fun about sports. Good athletes remain motivated to stay involved because they continue to get chances to participate as they move up the competitive ladder. For less skilled athletes, the chances become fewer and the fun becomes less and less.

Just getting the opportunity to swing the bat at the ball on the tee can be great fun for a five-year-old. By the time that same child is ten, other factors must come into play for the activity to remain fulfilling. Most important, the child must learn new skills.

Improvement and Skill Building

In my experience, this is *the* single most important factor driving children's involvement in sports. The need to build new skills must be fulfilled if children are to continue to be interested in and enjoy sports. Interestingly, in surveys that ask children why they *stopped* playing sports, the two main reasons given are "I lost interest" and "I was not having fun." Loss of interest and pleasure are the results of a stagnant sports experience. It is virtually impossible for children to lose interest if they are constantly learning and being challenged.

As young children grow and develop, they face a big challenge. They must answer the question, Who am I? Children cannot answer this question by referring to their career, as adults usually do. Instead, they must develop their own identities. They do this by discovering what makes them different from the other children with whom they socialize. An essential aspect of forging a unique identity is the process of mastering a variety of physical skills. A child must feel in control of his own body in order to have a general sense of confidence. From the earliest ages to adulthood, the need to keep improving and growing is the major reason that athletes stay in sports. Sport psychologists call this the "competence" motivation, but it is more simply described as the desire to be good at something. This desire is a powerful motivator.

 ## The Physical Thrill

Being able to use your body, go fast, become strong, jump, catch, hit, and run are fun for kids. As adults, we often yearn for the connection of mind and body, but children know the fun of integrating mind and body at an unconscious level. One young athlete I work with told me, "What I like most about cycling is going fast. I like racing fast." Another youngster admitted, "I play noseguard in school. I like the hitting part."

Clearly there can be great individual differences in what children find physically exciting. It's fun to expose children to a variety of sports and see which ones they take to. Although parents often wonder if a child is "talented" in a particular sport, I think that love of the sport has more to do with long-term success than talent. A child who loves baseball and will do anything to get a chance to play will get much more out of that sport than out of another—say, tennis—for which experts might tell him he is best suited.

 ## Friendships

As children become more social, sports provide an excellent setting for making friends and enjoying shared experiences. Team sports can provide a special thrill not often found in other life areas, where a group pulls together for a common cause. "I like the team," says a young athlete, "It feels good to work together." Another athlete comments, "I meet lots of people through sports. It's just fun."

The social benefits of sports change greatly during the child's development. For the young child, sports involvement might offer the opportunity to play with new friends, or to see schoolmates in a different setting. But by adolescence, belonging to a sports team may be a very significant experience, involving a complex web of relationships and friendships and offering the opportunity for identity as part of a special group. Karen, one of my clients, identifies herself as a member of the Eagles soccer team ahead of any other affiliation. Her best friends are on the team, they hang out together when not practicing, and they spend considerable time thinking about the team's goals and how to achieve them. Karen's identity is partially shaped by her team experience.

Social Recognition

Young athletes report that the attention and recognition they receive for being a good athlete can be rewarding. Rewards such as the tradition of "getting letters" in varsity school sports, or the trophies that are awarded at the end of travel tournaments, are often part of the sports system in both schools and private programs.

Young athletes can become smaller versions of professional sports stars, attaining the status of minicelebrities in their communities. They receive coverage in local newspapers, their photos appear in print, and sometimes they are even interviewed on television. Being a celebrity is an enjoyable experience for many young athletes, and those who don't attain such fame still bask in the glow of approval by family and friends. Of course, having a child who is a star athlete can also be very rewarding for parents.

The special status of being a good athlete can also bring life opportunities that might not otherwise be possible. For example, a team may make the national finals in an event, and the families might become involved in raising money to finance travel to the championships. Some of the very best young athletes even get to travel overseas on junior national teams, no doubt arousing the admiration, and perhaps jealousy, of their peers.

Competition

This aspect of fun is a two-edged sword. For some children, there is a great deal of enjoyment in measuring themselves against others. One athlete explained, "I'm fairly quick, and I just have fun going up against someone and trying to outdo them." But as children grow older, increasing competition can also become discouraging. Many athletes who come to see me mention the increasing pressure they feel as they move higher in their sport.

I have devoted an entire chapter (Chapter Seven) to understanding how competitive attitudes develop, and another to describing the role it plays, and should play, in children's youthful sporting experiences. But the bottom line is that children love to win games, whether tic-tac-toe or an organized game of baseball. Whether young children really understand what it means to win is another question.

Attention

Children like the attention they get from their parents when they participate in sports. This attention can be a powerful reinforcer for continued participation in a specific sport. For example, Matthew is a large, thoughtful ten-year-old who is good in school and has tried several sports. His father is a successful lawyer and has little time to spend with his three children. Matthew rarely sees his father at teacher conferences at school, and his father shows little interest in Matthew's school band or his swim team. But when Matthew joins a junior football program, his father manages to find time to come to most of the games and occasionally to help out at practices. Matthew doesn't find football as much fun as swimming or band—but how likely is he to drop the sport when he gets this much attention from Dad?

Another informative way to evaluate what older children and adolescents want out of their play experiences is to see what sorts of activities they choose to engage in when they are on their own.

HOW CHILDREN PLAY
WHEN THEY PLAY BY THEMSELVES

How do young people organize sports activities when adults aren't around? Think about the sorts of nonorganized physical activities you observe young people engaged in. What activities are they? Young people tend to play together in such activities as in-line skating, skateboarding, pickup basketball and football, bicycling, and so on. These are all examples of what Jay Coakley calls *informal* sports. They are characterized by being organized by the young players themselves.

I'm sure that many parents can empathize with the distinction between the high-pressure, overly controlled experiences of today's child playing in a wanna-be professional organized youth sports program, and their own experiences of happiness and involvement playing pickup games of football or baseball in a vacant lot or empty field. A wise little video called *Two Ball Games*, produced by Doug Klieber of the Department of Psychology at Cornell University, makes this point beautifully by juxtaposing a pickup game of softball with a Little League baseball game. On the one hand, using no voice-over, just pictures, the video shows parents at the organized game getting intense as they cheer on their little warriors, shows some children losing interest and some displaying anxiety, and shows how adults dictate all the rules to the children. On the other hand, the video shows children in the pickup game cooperating, shows conflicts resolved by do-overs, shows leaders emerging to help the group get organized, and shows children enjoying a game without worrying about winning or losing.

I've been associated with youth sports programs for more than thirty years and it often seems to me that an unintentional side-effect in adult-organized programs is to prevent children from playing. The sign-up procedures, need for uniforms, number of practices, competitive leagues, travel schedule, and coaching practices conspire to force many parents and children away from such programs. In contrast, the informal sports of children themselves are driven by a need to recruit as many participants as possible. And if youngsters start leaving the game, the game is over. So informal games are designed to get and keep everyone involved. Wouldn't it be great to transplant that philosophy into organized youth sports programs?

THE OBJECTIVES OF INFORMAL PLAY

Coakley and his colleagues have observed and monitored these informal games and interviewed the participants to find out how they feel about these activities. Coakley has found that across a spectrum of informal sports, young people are trying to achieve four main objectives:

- Action (the more, the better)
- Personal involvement (everyone plays as much as possible)
- Excitement (close scores in contests, exciting moves in noncontests)
- Friendships (the opportunity to interact with friends)

I believe that such research is extremely valuable, because it gives us a unique way of understanding the motivations and needs of young athletes. I have observed that when organized sports programs fail, they often fail to meet the needs of young athletes in one or more of these areas.

Action

Action is absolutely necessary for any game to be enjoyable. Children don't have much fun sitting around watching others play; they want to get out there themselves. Unfortunately, many organized competitive sports are structured in such a way that even the children who play aren't active. Just the other day I was watching a coed baseball game for eight-year-olds and I noticed that the little right fielder, who had been standing in the sun for ten minutes while the other team batted, had lost interest in the game and was wandering around picking wild flowers in the outfield. Sure enough, at that moment a line drive from the batter came racing in her direction, and the parents started jumping up and down yelling at her to get the ball. The sudden screams and yells completely confused her, and she went running in toward home plate, in the opposite direction of the ball. It was a funny moment, except that the young girl didn't appear to be enjoying herself after the incident. She was embarrassed by all the tumult, and a couple of the better players chastised her for costing the team two runs. I observed her sitting on the bench in the next inning with tears trickling down her face.

But watch children skateboarding together, and you see a continual flow of action, nonstop jumps, tricks, and flips. In pickup games of basketball there are no time-outs, free throws, or jump balls. The children keep the game flowing. Surely these informal sports can teach us some valuable lessons about how to structure sports for children.

Personal Involvement

Personal involvement is promoted in informal sports by means such as handicapping and rules changes. I remember, for example, that when we played baseball in a friend's backyard, one rule was "hit a home run and your team is out." This was because a home run meant the ball had cleared the fence and gone into a neighbor's yard, necessitating a game stoppage. Our rule gave the best players a chance to swing for the fences—but if they connected, the rule ensured that the other team then got its turn. In many informal games, according to Coakley, it is the less-skilled players who make most use of do-overs and interference calls in order to correct a mistake. This saves the less-skilled or younger players from the embarrassment of letting the team down or demonstrating their lack of prowess, and also keeps them involved in the action. More skilled or older players often end up being the team leaders or the unofficial game organizers, arbitrating arguments and so on. They are often informally rewarded for a stellar play or for an exciting move by the approval of the other players.

Excitement

Ask children to say what they find fun about the game they are playing and they will often name something specific such as hitting, catching, throwing, or running. It is through mastery of these skills that children build their physical self-esteem. Informal games emphasize such actions. Often the games are organized not to determine a winner but to promote spectacular, diving catches, long runs, deep throws, twisting shots, and other amazing tricks. This gives participants at all levels a chance to show off their skills. Excitement is built into informal sports. If scores are being kept, rule modifications are often allowed, serving to keep the game close and interesting to all involved. Teams may be allowed an extra possession if they are behind, good players may switch sides, new rules may be introduced, such as "the next score wins," and so on.

Friendship

The final objective for children playing informally is to spend time with friends. At this age, the definition of a friendship is choosing to play together. Informal sports give children a chance to interact, to learn about competing with one another, and perhaps to make new friends. Whereas in organized programs good friends often end up on different teams, or always competing, informal activities give children a chance to choose with whom they wish to play.

Looking at informal sports shows us that children do not need to play mini-versions of professional adult sports to have fun. When children organize their own sports, they emphasize participation, action, excitement, and friendships. Adults can increase the motivation of children to play sports by arranging sports programs that provide these outcomes. Also, parents must listen to the expressed individual needs of their own child. Clearly there are many possible reasons that children want to participate in youth sports. How can a parent or coach find out what a child expects or desires from her sports experience?

HOW DOES A PARENT KNOW WHAT A CHILD WANTS?

The best way to find out what a child wants is to ask. Good communication is the best way to prevent many of the problems we see in youth sports today.

To facilitate such communication, I have provided in Exhibit 4.1 a Youth Sports Motivation Survey, to be completed by young athletes. It provides them with an opportunity to examine twenty-eight possible reasons for participating in a sports program for children or adolescents, and to indicate which motives they endorse. It also asks the survey taker to indicate his or her top three reasons for engaging in an organized sports program.

Parents can use this survey to understand why their child is attracted to playing sports. Asking a child to fill out the survey and then examining the answers carefully is a good stepping stone to better communication. I have found that parents are often surprised by some of the reasons their child chooses.

Coaches can use this survey in a team environment to determine the major motives endorsed across the entire team. It is also a good idea, however, to look at some of the reasons chosen by just one athlete, or by just a few. This helps to emphasize that there can be great diversity in the motivations of the children participating. It may not be possible for one program to meet all the needs of all the children, but I believe that it is possible for a good program to satisfy many of these needs. In the next section I discuss how programs can be set up to meet the most common needs of youth sports participants.

Exhibit 4.1. Youth Sports Motivation Survey.

The following is a list of reasons that young people have given in answer to the question, Why do you play sports? Please look at each reason and decide how much you agree with it. If a reason is one for which you play your sport, place a mark in the box under "I agree." If it is not one of the reasons that you play your sport, place a mark in the box under "I do not agree." If you're not sure if it is a reason that you play your sport, place a mark in the box under "I'm not sure."

	I agree	I'm not sure	I do not agree
1 I can be active.	☐	☐	☐
2. I learn new skills.	☐	☐	☐
3. I can get better.	☐	☐	☐
4. It helps me be fit.	☐	☐	☐
5. It helps me be healthy.	☐	☐	☐
6. I make and have friends.	☐	☐	☐
7. It is exciting.	☐	☐	☐
8. My parents want me to play.	☐	☐	☐
9. I can win competitions.	☐	☐	☐
10. I'm good at it.	☐	☐	☐
11. It makes me feel special.	☐	☐	☐
12. It helps me with life.	☐	☐	☐
13. I have fun.	☐	☐	☐
14. I can be part of a team.	☐	☐	☐
15. It helps me look good.	☐	☐	☐
16. It gives me energy.	☐	☐	☐
17. I can compete against others.	☐	☐	☐
18. I learn about myself.	☐	☐	☐
19. It helps me get along with others.	☐	☐	☐
20. I learn self-control.	☐	☐	☐
21. It will help me be a good athlete.	☐	☐	☐
22. My friends want me to play.	☐	☐	☐
23. I will earn money for sports in the future.	☐	☐	☐

	I agree	I'm not sure	I do not agree
24. I will be chosen for a better team.	☐	☐	☐
25. It makes me feel good.	☐	☐	☐
26. It gives me confidence.	☐	☐	☐
27. I like this sport.	☐	☐	☐
28. I like my coach.	☐	☐	☐

Now, look over this list and write down the three most important reasons that you play your sport.

1. _____

2. _____

3. _____

It is important for coaches to describe the goals of their program in a manner that is understood by the young people who are participating. Whether it is young children playing in largely instructional leagues, or adolescents playing in competitive high school programs, the young athletes deserve to know what they can expect from the program they have joined. Having clear goals is part of the job of a coach. A coach who has a well-thought-out philosophy of coaching has addressed his or her expectations of the benefits that participants will receive.

CREATING GOOD YOUTH SPORTS PROGRAMS

To overcome the dark side of youth sports, it is extremely important, I think, for adults to understand the motivation of children who participate in athletic programs. Only if we know what children want out of a sports program can we design ones that meet their needs. It is also clear that programs that do not meet the needs of children will not attract participants. Young people quickly drop out of programs that fail to address their motivations. Good youth sport programs go beyond children's expectations and give young people experience that not only meets their needs but also gives them skills they didn't realize they needed. Good programs also begin by being intrinsically interesting and rewarding.

Thinking about the major factors that motivate children to participate in youth sports, it is easy to see the important implications for building a good youth sports program. Certain resources must be in place and certain factors must be considered in order to establish an effective sporting program for young people. Here are some ideas on what good youth sport programs can do for their children.

Start with Good Coaches

Many of the motives expressed by children in surveys of their needs can be satisfied only by the coach. It is the coach who makes important decisions about who plays and for how long, and it is the coach's responsibility to teach young athletes the skills they need to play a sport well. Good coaching is the decisive factor in determining the success of a youth sports program.

The influence of the coach on children's satisfaction with their sports experience has been demonstrated in research conducted by Frank Smoll and Ron Smith of the University of Washington. They followed the actions of fifty-one male Little League coaches over the course of a season and measured the effects on 542 young athletes on their teams. They found that the way coaches behaved during games had a decisive impact on the attitudes of the players toward the game. Young athletes responded much more favorably to coaches who were *supportive* of their players (reinforced correct skills and encouraged athletes who made mistakes) and *instructive* (taught players the basics and showed them how to correct their mistakes). Athletes who played for supportive and instructive coaches liked them more, were more likely to indicate that they would play Little League baseball next season, and even liked their team-mates better.

Despite our society's emphasis on being a winner, a fascinating finding of this research was that the win-loss record of the young athletes' teams did not influence how much the players liked their coaches or their sport. Simply put, being on a winning team or a losing team was not nearly as important as the type of coach the player had. Even more interesting, these players reported that they believed that their parents liked them more, and that their coach liked them more, when they played on a winning team rather than on a losing team. Even at a young age (these children were ages eight to fifteen), children learn that winning is more important to adults than it is to them.

Modify the Game When Appropriate

We need more youth sports programs that are willing to give children a chance to develop their physical abilities in creative and individualized ways. Playing adult versions of games with children as participants is not constructive. My eight-year-old daughter recently took up soccer, and her team plays what might be called "big clump soccer." I'm sure you have seen some version of it. Games consist of one child kicking the ball, her ten teammates running after her shouting for the ball, and the eleven children on the other team trying to tackle her. It's like watching a big clump of bodies roll around the field!

Games such as this are usually won by the team that has the fastest and strongest runners and kickers. I have observed the same phenomenon many times with junior football and basketball. Until about age eleven or twelve, children are not mentally equipped to understand difficult concepts such as teamwork and positional play. Attempts to force children into game structures that they don't understand and can't adhere to is likely to reduce the fun factor, a recipe for losing children as participants.

Programs that modify the rules to make the game more appropriate for that age group are more likely to keep children involved. Also, programs that teach young children the fundamentals via fun games and activities (not necessarily by playing competitive games) are doing the children a far greater service than programs that simply put children in teams and have them play each other. What sort of program is your child in?

Provide the Opportunity to Play

We lose children from sports when we let them sit around, waiting their turn or watching others. Although in some sports (such as basketball) the chance to take a break is built into the game and is often needed to give tired players a rest, in many youth sports programs the periods of inactivity are unnecessary. With some structural changes to the game, or with some rule modifications, it is possible to get everyone involved and to increase the activity level. T-ball is a good example of a modification to baseball that greatly increases the action level (hitting the ball) for those who are learning the game. Another example is lowering the height of the basketball hoop, which increases the action (making a basket) for smaller and younger children.

Introduce Competitions Gradually

One way in which many traditional youth sports programs fail to meet the needs of children is by introducing too much competition too early. Too much competition tends to retard skill development in sports. This observation is somewhat surprising, because those who advocate higher levels of competition in youth sports usually do so to promote talent development. After all, such common youth sports institutions as "age select," "all star," and "traveling" teams don't make much sense except from the perspective of identifying good athletes and giving them increased opportunities to receive good coaching and good competition. There are, however, a variety of reasons that playing a large number of competitive games is not a good method for helping children develop their sports skills to the fullest.

Competitions restrict participation. In many adult sports there are long periods of inactivity, such as between innings, or when the defense is on the field. Such inactivity is not appropriate for children. In many sports, tournaments and contests proceed through some process of elimination. Some teams or individuals win and get to play again, while others lose and stop playing. Even many nationwide youth sports programs that endorse the "everyone plays" philosophy violate this rule by sponsoring national competitions that systematically eliminate all teams but one—the eventual champion. Again, for younger athletes it is much more sensible to promote competitions that keep teams involved throughout the process. Winning tournaments is not nearly as important for six- to fourteen-year-olds as is helping these youngsters develop sound skills and encouraging them to strive to reach their potential.

Competitions tend to emphasize results instead of excellence. If a young athlete comes home and is asked, "Did you win?" she will quickly come to realize that the result of a contest is valued more highly than how she played or what she learned. Why keep score if the result doesn't matter? When competition is deemphasized for young athletes, it gives them and the adults involved (coaches and parents) the freedom to worry less about results and focus more energy on skill learning, creativity, and having fun.

Competitions can create high levels of anxiety. Researchers have found that many forms of competition involve some anxiety. One of the most important findings is that for some children this anxiety level is very high. When this is the case, it is difficult to learn and to retain skills, and difficult to perform skills well.

Children who find competitions to be anxiety provoking are less likely to stay in a sport. It is useful for all children to learn the skills to deal with anxiety in evaluative situations, and sports are excellent activities for teaching such skills. But until children learn these skills, adults should strive to minimize the anxiety felt by young athletes. More effective learning will take place when anxiety is kept low. Reducing the competitive nature of youth sports is a good way to reduce the anxiety for many young athletes.

Coaches tend to utilize a "star" rather than a "team" approach during competitions. Recently I hosted a work group of parents and coaches who were trying to establish the goals of their sports program and whether they should include winning as a goal. One of the parents in this debate made a good point: if children are placed in a competitive environment, they want to win. It's not as much fun to lose. Adults coaching such youth teams also want to win. It is hard for adults to see children become unhappy when they lose. Unfortunately, at the younger ages one of the best ways to ensure that your team will win is to involve your best players as much as possible. One or two stars can often win games single-handedly in youth sports competitions. It is therefore only natural for youth league coaches to want to play their stars as much as possible. So they do.

I have observed this pattern of focusing on the young stars so often across so many sports that I would venture to say that it is a behavior endemic to youth sports programs. It is a harmful behavior, however, and a good indicator of the crisis we face in organizing beneficial sports programs for children.

Focusing on a few stars does little for the talent development of the other, nonstar players. If they are given fewer opportunities to participate, they have fewer learning opportunities. Many parents have cited their frustration at seeing a few favored athletes receive the bulk of attention as a major reason for taking their child out of a youth sports program.

Paradoxically, these extra opportunities to play and win may also hurt the development of the young star athletes. Such precocious youngsters often excel at an early age thanks to their early maturation and to factors such as speed, coordination, and strength. Reliance on these talents often diminishes the attention the young stars pay to skill development and technique, which comes back to hurt them as they grow older and encounter more competition. Studies indicate that very few age-group stars ever end up being successful in professional or Olympic sports. In fact, there are many examples of athletes who were ignored by youth sports programs and schools when they were young who later developed into outstanding athletes, such as David Robinson and Isaiah Thomas.

It makes the most sense, therefore, for coaches to resist the tendency to focus on their star athletes and to help all participants develop as well as they can in sports. In excellent sports programs, the adults concerned discuss this issue, set goals based on true development of skills, and educate participants concerning the benefits of such a focus.

There are no opportunities for mistake correction and rehearsal during competition. A final reason that competitive sports often hurt skill development is that they limit learning opportunities. Good coaches know that the best way to correct an athlete's mistake is to show the athlete the right way to do it and to have them try again. When children's sports programs are conducted on an adult model, there are no opportunities for do-overs or mistake corrections. Parents think, "Tiger Woods doesn't stop the game and ask for a chance to try a bad shot again, so why should our children?" But of course there is a huge difference between Tiger Woods, an expert who has already mastered his skills and who is playing in very competitive events, and the situation of most children, who are still trying to learn and who play with other children who are trying to learn.

There are programs that take a learning approach within organized competitions for children and that give children the opportunity to learn from mistakes and make corrections. Indeed, the good news for youth sports is that there are many wonderful programs that do a great job of meeting the needs of young people. We need more like them.

Emphasize Social Interaction

Children like to play games because it gives them a chance to make friends, be with their friends, and play with and compete against their friends. Too often, adults miss opportunities to enhance the social aspects of youth sports programs.

Most professional leagues encourage the oppositional nature of sports. In fact, the language of professional sports is often military— "it was a real war out there," "it was a battle all the way, but I eventually triumphed," and "we were on the attack from the start, but they put up a great fight." It is hard to see your opponent as a friend if he is considered your enemy, but children are looking for a social experience in sports.

As adults, we can maximize the social aspects of sports by promoting interaction among team members and between teams. Introducing players to one another before every contest, holding occasional social events after games or tournaments, and insisting that players shake hands during contests and after arguments or fights are all examples of ways in which adults can simply and easily maximize the social benefits that sports offer. Once this becomes an established goal of a youth sports program, the opportunities for affirming friendships and teaching social skills are myriad.

Provide Variety and Interest

Even when youth sports programs involve a lot of action, they can fail children, especially younger children, if they don't provide excitement or stimulation. My own personal experience with a traditional program failing in this manner occurred when I became involved in a youth swimming program with my then seven-year-old son, Bryan. Since his earliest days he has loved the water. I'm not sure if it's the Australian genes he inherited from me or the constant exposure we gave him to swimming at local YMCA's and town pools, but he has never shown any fear of water and has been a fast learner in all his swimming groups. As he grew older, I investigated local swimming programs and found one that seemed ideal for him. Not only did it offer an increased level of instruction, but it would also gradually introduce him to swimming competitions. I asked Bryan if he wanted to join and he jumped at the chance. He was asked to go to a "selection trial" to see if he had sufficient skills to enter the program, and on the day of his trial he was nervous and excited. When he was told he could join the program he was ebullient, as only a seven-year-old can be.

From the outset I realized that Bryan wasn't getting the teaching he needed to continue to improve. The main problem was the scarcity of coaches. With fifty children in the program and only two coaches, there just wasn't enough time to help each child. Making matters worse, the coaches stayed on the sides of the pool, shouting vague verbal instructions to six-, seven-, eight-, and nine-year-olds! Children at this age need demonstrations to learn. But the coaches never entered the water with the children, missing a great teaching opportunity.

Still, I hoped that the opportunity to swim with other children his own age would be attractive to my son. At first it seemed to be enough. Bryan didn't complain, and he dutifully did whatever the coaches told him. Over the next few weeks, however, I noticed his enthusiasm diminish. The excitement and eagerness to swim were gradually disappearing. Still, I persevered.

Suddenly, during one especially boring drill that consisted of swimming up and down every lane in the pool, Bryan's motivation crumbled. He climbed out of the pool and walked over to me. In tears, he asked, "Do I have to keep doing this? I hate it." The intensity of his reaction caught me by surprise. Sure, I had noticed that he wasn't as excited about swimming as he had been, but hate? Without pausing to consider, I put my arm around him, grabbed his towel, and left the pool with him. I knew instinctively that pushing him to continue would turn him against an activity he loved.

So we left the world of organized youth swimming and returned to the local pools and beaches. Bryan still loves swimming. But I wonder how many other children we drive away from wonderful, interesting activities every year because our instructional programs bore them to tears.

I know many parents worry over the decision to allow a child to drop out of an organized sports program. A common concern is that allowing a child to drop out teaches him to be a "quitter." Let me assure parents that there is no evidence to suggest that allowing children to leave sports programs in which they are unhappy leads to adult problems with commitment. However, the question of when to allow a child to leave a program and when to encourage them to stay is a good one. When counseling parents who have this question, I suggest that they be flexible and understanding in their approach. I see problems arising when parents try to stick to a rigid approach, such as never allowing a child to quit. When children are young, it makes sense to encourage them to try sports, even when they might initially be fearful or anxious. But it doesn't make sense to keep a nine-year-old in a program she actively dislikes, because she is probably too young to understand any lessons about long-term commitment.

Once children develop the intellectual capacities to understand that when they sign up for a program, they should be committed to it, I suggest that it is appropriate to set up negative contingencies for leaving the program. For example, a parent might pay the sign-up fee for a karate course if the child completes the program, but if she drops out, the child pays the sign-up fee out of her allowance. Usually, children are in the early secondary school years when they develop sufficient intellectual capacities to understand that effort, preparation, commitment, perseverance, practice, and study are required to be successful and to fully enjoy an organized sports program.

Provide Close and Exciting Contests

Children playing by themselves usually find a way to make their contests close and exciting. Adults, sometimes with the best of intentions, often find ways to make contests boring. For example, one of the strangest rules I have ever encountered in youth sports is the "ten run rule" or its equivalent. Used in many youth sports games such as junior baseball, the idea is that when two youth teams are playing, if one team is ahead by ten runs or more at the end of an inning, the game ends. I can't think of a better example of how to organize a boring game.

It has been pointed out to me that such rules prevent children from being humiliated. But what is wrong with the way we structure games for children if they allow the prospect of humiliation? I suppose the idea behind the rule is to make sure that very lopsided games are not continued beyond the point when anyone would find them interesting. But what message are we sending to the children in such games? How would you feel if you were playing golf on the weekend and all your group walked off the course at the thirteenth tee because you were playing so badly? Or your tennis partners quit when the score was four to zero because they were too far ahead? I think the only message that children receive in such a situation is that competitive sports can be boring and silly. There are so many alternatives to rules such as this. Instead of ending the game, or even starting a new one, players could be swapped between teams, the team behind could be given some extra outs or an extra inning, different pitchers could be used, the coaches and umpires could help children who are having difficulties, and so on.

In some ways, understanding the motives of children who play sports is the easiest step in working to create programs that truly meet the needs of children. It is often far harder to explain the motives of parents who pressure their child into playing an undesirable sport, or who take risks with the health and safety of their child in pursuit of some elusive dream of success.

ESCAPING THE PARENT TRAP

*Pushing Your Own Dreams or
Encouraging the Young Athlete?*

It is no easy task to be the parent of a young athlete. Hard enough are the tasks of helping the child learn how to handle the ups and downs of competition. But perhaps most challenging are the demands on the parent's *own* coping skills—learning how to manage emotions that are repeatedly tested under trying conditions. Parents often receive the advice, for example, to stay cool and detached and to just let their child have fun while competing. "Shut up, sit down, watch the game quietly, and let the kid have fun," enjoins one book for parents. But how, exactly, can parents remain objective about such a subjectively involving experience?

The youth sport experience is seductive. Parents can begin with the best intentions, hoping to give their child an enjoyable and worthwhile experience. But it is important to recognize that watching one's own child compete begins to tap into the needs of parents to see their child succeed and be happy. Parents experience a rush of positive emotions when their child triumphs, a deflating sense of emptiness when they lose. This emotional process can become almost addicting. Instead of focusing on the child's goals, parents can get caught up in seeking more experiences where they can feel that rush of positive emotions. They can begin to focus on their own fantasies for their child—fantasies of success, fame, and recognition.

THE PARENT TRAP

Some of the parents I have worked with have described the experience of youth sports almost like someone talking about an addiction. Mary was a "skating parent" for more than ten years in Colorado Springs. For more than a decade she came to nearly every practice, traveled the country to attend her daughter's competitions, organized countless fundraising activities, and sewed many dresses. "I got hooked the first time I saw Tess on the medal stand," she explains. "I can't describe the feeling. It made me feel so proud and feel so good for her. I always wanted her to be happy, and she was always so happy whenever she won an event."

Mary pauses before continuing. "What you don't realize is how it pulls you in. I kept coming back for more. Winning an event was never enough. There were always better competitions to enter, tougher opponents to face. After a while I stopped listening to Tess. I wanted her to win. For me, I think. I needed it. The last few years were pretty bad. Tess wanted out a long time before I realized that it had to be that way. She was angry with me for the last few years. I just hope I didn't waste her childhood."

Mary is describing a common problem for parents—their love of their child leads them to behave in ways that ultimately hurt the child's development, or hurt their relationship. A parent's positive and natural instincts somehow become distorted through the competitive experience, and the parent loses the ability to make wise decisions. In fact, many of the athletes I have counseled have told me they feel as though their parents begin acting like children. It is as though the youth sports process brings out the worst in many of us.

Joe, a burly football player on a local college team, told me about his experience when he was twelve years old. "I was on a youth league baseball team, and my father was the coach. He was always a yeller—it was embarrassing to me. But the worst was one day when we got to a game and the other coach wanted to play with the 'short center fielder' rule, which is where you have ten players on the field. My Dad didn't want to do it. He said league rules forbid it. The other coach said that all the coaches he knew did it, it helped get more kids in the game. My Dad started yelling. They were face-to-face for twenty minutes, arguing with each other. Finally my Dad told us the game was canceled. We all had to go home. It was the saddest thing. Here were thirty-five kids with their gloves and bats waiting to play on a beautiful day and we had to go home because two adults were acting like little kids."

The paradox of being a parent is that the good reasons we have for pushing our children to succeed can lead to behaviors that instead teach our children to be selfish and grasping. Unfortunately, parents get caught in this trap all the time. Parents naturally identify with their child, but overidentification causes parents to ignore their child's feelings and focus on their own. Parents dream of their child's future but sometimes get so attached to their own dreams that they lose sight of what the child wants. Parents love their children so much that they make tremendous sacrifices on their behalf, spending money to support the child's sport and taking time to be there for the child. However, parents can come to see these sacrifices as investments and then expect that the investments will pay off and yield tangible benefits. Parents want their child to excel but can get caught up in competing with other parents, pushing their child to succeed and hoping that the other children will fail, giving their child a chance to shine.

The dilemma for those who run youth sports programs is that programs that can do so much good can also bring out the worst in some parents and coaches. How can we promote the positive aspects of youth sports while weeding out the dark side?

Watching parents who do a great job of supporting their child's development in sports, and watching those who fall into the trap of pushing their child beyond the limits, I have seen that the difference is whether parents can put their own desires aside and focus on what their child needs. This is no easy task. Parents identify very strongly with their children, but it is overidentification that causes the problems. It is often difficult to tell when that line has been crossed. That is why parents struggle all the time with the issue of how much they should push their child. It's good to encourage a child to persevere in learning a new skill, especially when the child initially fails. But if encouragement becomes cajoling, then bribing, and then threatening the child, the line has been crossed.

Bill, a large, warm-hearted man, is typical of parents struggling with this issue. Now a successful plumber, Bill was an all-around sports star in school and excelled in basketball, football, and baseball. As we talk, he constantly displays his affection for his son Matt, tousling his hair and patting him on the shoulder as he speaks. Matt, age seven, sits politely throughout our meeting, but he often has a dreamy look on his face, as if he's thinking of something else.

"I just don't know if I should give up or not" explains Bill. "I got so much out of sports when I was a kid, I really wanted Matt to have those opportunities, too," he says. "But he just doesn't seem interested. I put him in T-ball when he was five, and later that year he started football, and last year he played in the town recreational basketball program. Nothing. He's not interested, he doesn't seem keen to go to the games, he never talks to me about them. A lot of the time he says he doesn't want to go, but I promise him a dollar or maybe an ice cream if he'll just give it another try." Bill stares with obvious love but concern at Matt. "Am I pushing him too hard?" he asks. "He's good at school, he loves to read. Maybe he's just not an athlete. I just wanted to talk to you and see what you think, Doc," he tells me. "Should I give up on sports for Matt?"

In our achievement-oriented society, these are serious issues for parents. When to push, when to lay back? How hard to push, how easy to take it? Which way is the right way?

In this chapter I examine how parents can separate their own goals from those of their child. Parents can avoid the parent trap by focusing on helping their child be self-reliant. They succeed when they encourage their child's sports goals. They fail when they push a child to fulfill the parent's dreams and ambitions. The behavior of parents is the focus of this chapter. In Chapter Six, I explore the effects of the youth sports experience on the whole family.

A Father's Dreams

Jay Morrow is a caring, loving father, who fell into the parent trap. His struggle to escape from the trap is the best illustration of the dangers of overidentification with a young athlete, and of how parents can learn to put their own ambitions aside and focus on their child.

There was a palpable tension among Jay's family when they walked into my office. This is something I have come to expect from families who are having difficulties with a child's sporting participation. Usually the greatest tension is between one of the parents and a child athlete. Other family members often take sides with one of the principals. In this case, Jay seemed to be lined up against his daughter, Susan, and his wife, Patti.

Susan was a starting player on the girls varsity volleyball team at a local high school. Jay was a successful education professional in New York City and had been a very good athlete in high school, starring on his school's baseball team. The conflict between Jay and Susan began over Jay's attempts to help Susan improve her volleyball skills. Susan had begun to play volleyball at age fourteen, and within a year had displayed enough signs to be earmarked by local coaches as "talented." Jay was delighted at Susan's success. With three daughters, Jay had begun to believe that he would never experience the joy of a child playing a team sport at a high level. Susan's two older sisters, Rachel and Jessica, had both been good at running. One competed in track, and the other specialized in cross-country running. Jay always encouraged their active sports participation, but inside he was a little disappointed that they showed no interest in such sports as softball or soccer. When Susan began to excel in volleyball, he was very pleased.

Although he knew little about the game initially, Jay purchased some training guides and read as much as he could about the techniques and strategies of volleyball. He began to work with Susan after school to help her improve her ball control skills. At first Susan enjoyed these times with her father. She received his undivided attention, and she was proud of the rapid development of her skills. Once she got to high school, however, Susan told me, her father's persistent interest in her volleyball became stifling. More outspoken than either of her sisters, Susan started to experience open conflict with her father. The conflict reached a head when Jay was appointed to be an assistant coach for the high school volleyball team. According to Susan, he was constantly offering advice about her game, and she didn't want it.

In her freshman year, Susan's on-the-court performance had been sensational. Her team had reached the finals of the state playoffs, and she was named to every all-star team. Jay brought in a large folder of press clippings about Susan from a variety of newspapers, documenting her volleyball career. In her sophomore year, her team again advanced to the state championship, but her individual statistics were not as impressive as those of her team members. Then, in her junior year, there was a marked decline in the press coverage. Jay showed me these pages sadly. "I don't know what's wrong with her these days," he commented. "She doesn't have the killer instinct anymore. You can see it in her body language when she's on the court. She's just not as confident as she used to be." Jay shook his head and looked at me.

All the Opportunities I Didn't Have

After meeting with the family on several occasions, I met with Jay alone a few times. During these meetings I had a chance to connect with Jay and learn more about his hopes and expectations for Susan. Jay was very much an overachiever. Born into a large family, with seven siblings, he endured a difficult childhood with an alcoholic father and a mother who held several jobs but still struggled financially. Jay was befriended during high school by a priest at the parochial school he attended, and he was encouraged to set his goals higher, both academically and athletically. As a result, he went to college after high school, the first in his family to do so. Although college was difficult for him, he persisted and earned his degree in history. Jay played baseball at college and was a decent pitcher—good enough to try his hand at semiprofessional ball when he graduated. But after three years of constant traveling and living out of a suitcase, Jay got tired of this life and sought security by joining the military.

Jay married while in the service and upon his discharge took a high school teaching position. His family grew and so did his career. He was a successful teacher and later moved into administration, although he said that "it is the hands-on work with kids I really love." But after turning fifty Jay became increasingly depressed. He felt that his relationship with his wife Patti had become "cold and distant," and he was disenchanted with administrative work. In our meetings his posture mirrored his mood. Jay sat slumped in a chair during our sessions, his eyes usually downcast, and he radiated an air of despair.

Except when he spoke about Susan and her volleyball. Then he would sit up, become animated, punching the air for emphasis with short, swift movements. Jay's great hope was that his children would have "all the opportunities I didn't have." He wanted them to feel secure at home and to be confident in their goals. Already his two older daughters, Rachel and Jessica, were in college. He was proud of them, but his hopes for Susan were even grander. He believed she had the talent to go to a big-name sports school out west, and his greatest hope was that a scholarship to play volleyball would unlock for her the door to these prestigious institutions. "Imagine Susan on a full scholarship at Stanford or Arizona," he would say wistfully, no doubt recalling his childhood days growing up in the inner city with little guidance and less hope. But now that dream was in jeopardy. "If Susan doesn't turn it around in her senior year," Jay explained, "she is not going to/get a full ride. Some of the big schools are still interested in her, but it's nearly too late. She's throwing her big chance away."

Jay's dreams for Susan were vivid and motivating. They were not shared by Susan. When I spoke to her alone, she had a different view of her future. She was much more confident than her father about her academic abilities. Her goal was to graduate high school with a high grade point average and go to college to study business. When I asked her about the school she would like to attend, she described a small, friendly, liberal arts college and named several of her top choices—none of them the big-league sports schools that Jay had set his heart on. I inquired as to the role she saw volleyball playing in her future. Susan was noncommittal.

"I like playing volleyball," she replied. "But I don't think I have the motivation to be a big-time college player. I know I've been very successful at the high school level, and that Dad wants me to go to Arizona State, but I don't think I want to work that hard. Last summer I went to a volleyball camp out West. All the top high school prospects were there. They really *wanted* it. They were *fierce* about volleyball. I'm not like that. I'd like to play, but only if I enjoy it. And I don't need a volleyball scholarship to go to college. I might even be able to get an academic scholarship if things go well."

Susan had her dreams, but getting a scholarship to play volleyball in college wasn't one of them. She resented the pressure she felt from her father to pursue his dream of athletic success. The result was a strained father-daughter relationship, full of tension and occasional confrontations.

Changing Channels: From Dreams to Reality

To help Jay really hear what Susan was saying, he needed to lessen his fixation on his dream of his daughter's stellar volleyball career. I worked with Jay on changing the way he talked to himself. He began to monitor how often he thought about Susan, worrying that she was "throwing it all away," fretting that she would "miss her big chance" to get a scholarship. Even Jay was surprised to realize how these thoughts preoccupied him. Initially Jay found that he spent some time *every hour* during the day worrying about Susan's volleyball performances.

I encouraged Jay to "change channels" when he noticed that he was worrying about Susan. Instead, he tried thinking about his *relationship* with Susan. Did he know what she wanted out of volleyball? What did she want from him? Such thoughts forced Jay outward, toward his daughter and away from his own dreams of glory.

This tactic—of encouraging the individual to identify the focus of their private thoughts and to try to change that focus, if necessary, to other, more important, issues—is one I use frequently. It is derived from an approach to counseling called *cognitive therapy*. Sometimes it sounds simplistic, but it is actually difficult to learn to do well. Some clients never learn how to change channels. It took Jay a couple of months to be able to identify when he was wasting energy worrying about his goals for Susan, and another month to begin to exert enough control that he could change these thoughts to productive issues concerning his relationship with Susan.

I challenged Jay to think about what his future relationship with Susan might be like. At first he drew a total blank. When he looked at his relationship with his other daughters, he realized that they were not close. Without volleyball to hold them together, he sensed that he and Susan might also drift apart. This was a difficult time for Jay. He became very depressed, and on several occasions at team practice he lost his temper with Susan. Twice he ended up verbally berating his daughter when they returned home after a game. This alienated Patti, who was protective of Susan. Jay apologized for his behavior during his sessions with me, but at first he had difficulty controlling his anger toward Susan.

Susan, on the other hand, seemed to grow more self-assured and relaxed with every week. During our times together I encouraged her to discuss with her father her own hopes for her college years. Perhaps sensing the support from her mother, Susan became increasingly assertive about her focus in her senior year of high school. She did not want her life to be dominated by volleyball. She continued to play at a high level, but she focused her college preparation on the types of liberal arts colleges into which she hoped to be accepted. Scholarships to play volleyball were not a high priority for her.

Gradually Jay was able to find other activities he could enjoy with Susan, including helping her research her college applications and taking more interest in her creative writing, which was very good. His sense of panic that volleyball would disappear and leave nothing behind seemed to ebb. Jay was able to change channels when he began worrying about Susan, realizing that his worries were founded on his own expectations, not on those of his daughter. But Jay remained somewhat depressed about his personal life and wondered where his career was going. As we ended our counseling sessions as a family, I suggested to Jay that he seek some individual counseling to deal with the personal issues that had arisen—especially the state of his marriage—after he had successfully confronted his conflict with Susan.

STEPPING OVER THE EDGE:
HOW PARENTS ENTER THE DARK SIDE

One of the themes I have consistently encountered in my work with athletes is that parents are seen both as a source of tremendous support and as a source of great stress. Often this perception is related to the current performance of the athlete. When things aren't going well, I often hear about the problems with parents. But when the athlete is achieving consistent success, she is usually happy to credit her parents with the support she needed to reach the top.

Sport psychologist Jon Hellstedt, who has spent many years researching the dynamics of athletic families, calls this the central paradox of the family of the young athlete. Their greatest strength—their unwavering emotional support of their child and their willingness to make sacrifices for the child's athletic advancement—is also their greatest weakness. The tremendous love and support of parents for their young athletes can sometimes help a talented child achieve great success, and can sometimes push a talented child to rebel and burn out. There is a fine line between encouraging a child to be achievement oriented and applying excessive pressure. Hellstedt suggests that the personality of the child may play a role in deciding whether the outcome is positive or negative: "What some young athletes see as parental encouragement might feel like a lack of freedom and breathing space to others." But I believe that a greater role is played by the parent's ability to remain relationship-focused rather than become self-absorbed. Overidentification is the process that drives parents into displaying the dark-side behaviors we dislike in youth sports.

I think there is always some ambivalence about the role played by parents in a child's achievements. I got my first inkling that this was an important issue even for successful athletes in the late 1980s. A graduate student, Othon Kesend, and I carried out a research project that involved interviewing forty-six elite athletes preparing for the 1988 Summer Olympic Games. Although 95 percent of these athletes said that their parents were their main source of encouragement in sports, a large percentage also said that their parents were a source of stress to them. These athletes could cite many examples of being supported and encouraged by parents through difficult times, but they could also point to occasions when their parents were critical and doubting. Thirty-five percent of the athletes said that their mother discouraged them at times, and 25 percent mentioned their father as a source of discouragement. One Olympian recalled, "I didn't understand my dad's harsh attitudes. I just wanted to go out and have fun, basically, and of course my dad wanted me to go out there and kick ass and take names. That took all the fun out of it. That meant that you had to be mad all the time and I didn't want to play like that."

It is not just athletes who experience failure or disappointment who experience difficulties with their parents. Even the very successful athletes we interviewed at times felt pressured by their parents. There seems to be a line that parents cross, such that on one side the actions of parents are seen as supportive and encouraging but on the other side their actions are seen as controlling and manipulating. Let's take a look at some of the typical behaviors we see from parents of young athletes, and observe how intentions to be supportive can become examples of applying too much pressure.

The Positive Side: Encouragement

Shouting out praise for a good play or in joy or excitement when a goal is scored or the child gets a base hit is a natural response for any parent. Indeed, the excitement generated at a youth sporting contest is one of the reasons for the popularity of youth sports.

Make no mistake, being a parent of a young athlete can require an enormous commitment in terms of time and energy. Many youngsters discover a game they love, and then it is up to the parents to support that interest by getting the child involved, providing coaching, buying equipment, organizing transportation to games and practices, and providing encouragement when the young athlete hits a roadblock.

To document the extent of the influence of parents on good athletes, researcher Grant Hill surveyed 152 baseball players who had made it into baseball as part of a professional rookie league. A majority of the athletes reported that when they were young their parents

- Provided money to buy equipment

- Regularly attended their baseball games

- Provided money for team fees and clinic costs

- Provided them with spending allowances during high school

- Accompanied the young players to see major or minor league baseball games

- Advised the players to pursue professional baseball careers

- Regularly practiced baseball with the young athletes

- Served as coach on one or more of the players' youth baseball teams

Clearly these athletes could not have made it to the professional ranks without the support of their parents. It is important to keep in mind that the majority of parents are strong supporters and encouragers of their children's athletic participation.

The Dark Side: The Overinvolved Parent

Unfortunately for the parent, these natural expressions of joy and excitement are often viewed negatively by observers who do not have a child in the contest. In his well-known book *No Contest*, for example, author Alfie Kohn deplores "the excessive competitive-ness of children's athletic programs, such as Little League baseball. The spectacle of frantic, frothing parents humiliating their children in their quest for vicarious triumph is, of course, appalling. . . ."

Which brings up the question, do parents who support their child from the sidelines provide encouragement or distraction for the child? What does the young athlete think about having Mom and Dad in the stands watching? The answer is that, overwhelm-ingly, children feel supported by having their parents present at competitions. Lauren, a teenage field hockey player, told me about her experiences as a young child playing soccer. "My parents didn't miss a game. They were at every game watching me, and that meant a lot to me." The majority of children feel loved and supported by their parents' presence at games.

Unfortunately, in some families the presence of Mom and Dad on the sidelines causes tension in the family. Often this is a result of a child who is self-conscious and therefore reacts negatively to extra attention. But sometimes it is due to the parents acting in ways that upset the young athlete, or that upset the coaches or officials. When this occurs, it can create tension not only for the family but also for all the children on the field, and often for all the parents watching. These tension-producing situations, although they are in the minority, tend to give parents on the sidelines a bad name. People tend to remember their negative experiences.

Even when a young athlete feels encouraged and supported by her own parents, the behavior of other parents can ruin the experience for them. "It wasn't even my own parents," said one nineteen-year-old client, "it was other parents screaming at the coach and at the referee that made most games a misery." This is a major problem for many youth sports programs. Recently I was asked to consult with a youth sport organization whose officials had found it necessary to cancel three games because of the behavior of parents on the sidelines. In two of the cases, the parents were cursing at children *on their own team*!

The Positive Side: Providing Constructive Criticism

Parents are in a good position to offer constructive criticism to their young athlete. After all, they have the potential to see their child playing far more often than the coach. And the way for a child to improve is to recognize his mistakes and correct them. Thus many parents provide early coaching for their child. It is very common for a parent to teach a child new skills if the parent also played the child's sport. What father, for example, would stand idly by if he saw his child holding a baseball bat the wrong way? The father will certainly jump in and show the child the right way to hold it.

Children can have a great deal of fun playing with their parents. A girl playing catch with her father, a young boy riding his bike with his mother—both are enjoying themselves and also learning physical skills. Skill building of this kind can take place in an informal way, free of the structure of an organized sports program. It is more challenging when a parent becomes a coach for a son's or daughter's youth sport team. Even in that situation, many parents are able to help their child learn and enjoy the game. The only advice I would offer on coaching your own child is to remember that a parent can easily make the distinction between being a parent and being a coach. However, children can't easily distinguish between criticism from "Dad the coach" versus "Dad the parent." For a child, the criticism is always coming from Dad. Thus children tend to be more sensitive to criticism from a parent-coach than from a nonparent coach.

The Dark Side: The Pushy Parent

Problems can arise when a parent's natural tendency to be supportive and to offer advice clashes with the coaching process in youth sports. Coaches, for example, are likely to see coaching behaviors by parents as intrusions. The greater the skill level of the young athlete, the more likely it is that the coach will have this perception. Consider how easy it is to put the child in a no-win position if the enthusiastic parent yells out some critical advice to her daughter from the stands. What if this advice differs from what the child was told by the coach? Who does the child try to obey? Her mother or the coach?

This is actually a common occurrence. I was speaking to a high school basketball coach recently who told me of many incidents where he tries to encourage the team to play sound positional strategy, only to hear parents telling a perimeter player to "take it to the basket, Jessie," or encouraging a player in a defensive role to "shoot the darn ball!" The coach's strategy was ruined by the well-meaning behavior of the parents.

The trouble with a parent offering critical advice is that the child may view it negatively. Most of the young children I see don't complain about their parents helping them learn the game, but many of the older children see their parents' advice-giving as unwelcome. Many of the thirteen- and fourteen-year-olds I talk to are frustrated by a father or mother who offers constant criticisms of their sports performance. The parent often sees himself as a great resource for his child, helping the child to learn the nuances of the game, but the child very often sees a parent who cares not about him but about how well he plays. This can be the beginning of a problem that is common in athletes as they reach late adolescence:

they see themselves only as athletes and evaluate their entire self-worth on the basis of how well they play.

The Positive Side: The Parent as Role Model

A good way for a child to learn the skill of self-control is by watching a parent display good self-control skills. Because organized youth sports programs often involve competitions, they frequently offer parents good chances to model for children effective ways of dealing with conflict. Handling a dispute over a clash in game schedules, deciding on who plays in what position, making a tough call in a close game—such situations abound in youth sports, and a parent or coach who remains calm and thoughtful in such situations provides the young athletes with an appropriate role model for handling emotional situations. Children learn far more from their observations of adult behavior than they do from verbal instructions on how to behave.

The Dark Side: The Abusive Parent

Shelley, a quiet and thoughtful fourteen-year-old, came with her father, Joe, to see me because he thought a sport psychologist might be able to help her with her attitude on the basketball court. Joe told me that Shelley lacked the competitive fire and that she was capable of playing basketball at a much higher level than she was demonstrating on the court.

Shelley and I met several times and talked about her feelings about basketball and about her approach to the game and to life. She was very clear that she didn't want to become more competitive. She loved the game, loved learning new moves, knew all the details about the players on the local ABL team, but didn't want to look at her opponents as the enemy in order to play well. Shelley felt intimidated by her father's presence at her basketball games. Especially galling to her was his attitude toward officials. He could often be heard shouting at them from the stands after a call had gone against Shelley or her team, and once Shelley recalled an official stopping the game and walking over to where her father sat and saying something to him. She was appalled. Shelley wondered how her father's actions made sense in light of his philosophy that all his children should respect authority and listen respectfully to their elders.

"It's all a bunch of crap, what he says," Shelley told me one day. "He has no respect for authority, but he expects me to toe the line. And when I say something about it, he yells at me."

Shelley's plight demonstrates the problems a parent's behavior can cause when it contradicts a parent's words. Parents can tell children about displaying self-control and respecting authority, but all their efforts are undermined if the child sees her parent get emotional at a sporting contest. As we well know, actions speak louder than words, particularly to children. Trouble begins when parents transfer the sort of fan behavior which is appropriate at professional sporting contests (such as yelling at players and criticizing an official for a perceived lousy call) to youth sports contests. The fact that more and more youth sports mimic professional events makes it more likely that parents will act like fans during games.

As parents sometimes painfully learn, when your own child is one of the sporting contestants, acting as a fan can have serious repercussions. I have seen many families in which a great deal of tension existed between a parent and a child athlete because of such actions by a parent. Often, too, parents are divided as one parent sides with the child on this issue while the other struggles to justify his or her behavior.

These are some specific examples of ways in which parents are trapped by the role they play in supporting a child athlete. Parents feel justified in acting in ways that are often perceived as controlling, negative, or confrontational. It is indeed a paradox. The question is, Is there any way out of it?

THE WAY OUT OF THE PARENT TRAP

I don't believe there is any way to avoid the emotional pressure that parents feel when they support their young athlete. As the athlete improves and faces higher levels of competition, this pressure naturally increases. The temptation for the parent to step over that fine line, to become overinvolved, will always be there. Sometimes it just seems easier to solve the problem for your child than to support their efforts to solve it on their own.

But I do believe that parents can learn to change their behaviors, so that they do not give in to the emotional pressure they feel but choose to act in a mature and responsible manner. Much of my counseling work with athletic families includes helping parents develop the skills to deal with the emotional pressures and learn how to pass these skills on to their child. The first step is to initiate open and honest communication between parents and the young athlete.

Talk to Your Child

In the previous chapter I provided the Youth Sports Motivation Survey so that parents could discover the motivations driving their children to participate in youth sports. It is also important for parents to consider what *they* expect their child will receive from participation. Over the years, I have found that a great deal of conflict between parents and coaches is due to fundamental differences in expectations concerning the program's goals. Parents have their own motivations for placing their child in an organized sports program. These motives should not be given a higher priority than those of the child, but they should be considered.

To help parents think about their own expectations of their child's involvement in sport, I have provided in Exhibit 5.1 a Youth Sports Motivation Survey for Parents. It gives parents an opportunity to examine twenty-eight possible reasons that their child might want to participate in a sports program for children or adolescents, and to indicate which motives they endorse. The survey taker is also asked to indicate the top three reasons why he or she wants the child to participate in an organized sports program.

I encourage the families I work with to discuss their answers to these questions. It can be very instructive for a young athlete to complete the Youth Sports Motivation Survey while his parents both complete the Youth Sports Motivation Survey for Parents. I encourage all three to sit down and compare their answers. Often there are some surprising differences, as well as some reassuring similarities.

When parents are devoting a great deal of time and energy to their child, they periodically need to look at themselves in the mirror. As parents, we must be honest and ask ourselves the tough questions. Am I overidentifying with my child? Am I placing her needs first? Am I really listening to her? Am I getting feedback from others that I am out of control, overcontrolling, pushy, or driving others crazy? Often talking to a spouse or a good friend can help give perspective and feedback that is so difficult to come by otherwise when you are intensely involved in your child's athletic career.

Once good communication has been established, it is easier to identify where potential problems might lie, and what to do about them. I suggest to all parents that they try to be role models for other parents who are struggling with the same pressures and emotions they are experiencing. I have encountered some unusual parents over the years who have demonstrated that the parent trap *can* be escaped with planning and with high levels of willpower.

I admire these parents because they are clearly swimming against the tide. The choices they make are often difficult, but perhaps due to some inner strength of conviction they are able to behave in ways that set them apart and enable them to enjoy their children's sports participation to the fullest. These parents do a wonderful job of raising children who have faith in their own abilities and who can cope independently with the challenges of life.

Here are some of the behaviors I have observed in parents who have broken the mold and managed to escape the clutches of the youth sports parent trap.

Exhibit 5.1. Youth Sports Motivation Survey for Parents.

The following is a list of reasons that parents often give for encouraging their children to participate in organized sports programs. Please look at each reason and decide whether it is why you believe your child should be involved in his or her sport. If it is a reason that you encourage your child to participate, place a mark in the box under "I agree." If it is not one of the reasons that you encourage your child to play his or her sport, place a mark in the box under "I do not agree." If you're not sure if it is a reason that you encourage your child to play his or her sport, place a mark in the box Under "I'm not sure."

	I agree	I'm not sure	I do not agree
1. To be active	☐	☐	☐
2. To learn new skills	☐	☐	☐
3. To get better	☐	☐	☐
4. To be fit	☐	☐	☐
5. To be healthy	☐	☐	☐
6. To make and have friends	☐	☐	☐
7. For excitement	☐	☐	☐
8. To stand out from other kids	☐	☐	☐
9. To win competitions	☐	☐	☐
10. To win scholarships	☐	☐	☐
11. To feel special	☐	☐	☐
12. To get help with life	☐	☐	☐
13. To have fun	☐	☐	☐
14. To be part of a team	☐	☐	☐
15. To look good	☐	☐	☐
16. To get energy	☐	☐	☐
17. To compete against others	☐	☐	☐
18. To learn about himself or herself	☐	☐	☐
19. To learn to get along with others	☐	☐	☐
20. To learn self-control	☐	☐	☐
21. To travel away from home	☐	☐	☐

	I agree	I'm not sure	I do not agree
22. To please friends who want him or her to play	☐	☐	☐
23. To prepare to earn money from sports in the future	☐	☐	☐
24. To be chosen for a better team	☐	☐	☐
25. To feel good	☐	☐	☐
26. To gain confidence	☐	☐	☐
27. Because he or she likes the sport	☐	☐	☐
28. Because he or she likes the coach	☐	☐	☐

Now, look over this list and write down the three most important reasons that you want your child to play his or her sport.

1. _____

2. _____

3. _____

Cheer for the Other Children

Parents who attend athletic competitions for children and focus obsessively on their child give a clear signal that they don't really care about the team or the event—they just care about their son or daughter. In contrast, parents who can be seen shouting and cheering for all the children on the team show that they have not fallen into the seductive narcissism of youth sports.

Two years ago I was working with the athletic director and the principal of a large regional high school who were frustrated by parents who seemed overly critical of the school's coaches and athletes. Spectators at the high school games could hear these parents shouting out critical comments about the limited playing abilities of other children on the team. The principal came up with the idea of sitting with the parents and organizing a cheering section for *all* the athletes on the team. Parents shouted words of praise to players who were being substituted, and words of encouragement to those entering the game. This simple idea worked very well. Perhaps because they looked silly being critical when the principal and other parents were so positive, the negative comments of the vociferous few faded away.

Take Time to Compliment the Officials

Even though many parents seem to feel that it is their inalienable right—perhaps even their duty—to criticize those who officiate at children's sports contests, the officials don't feel the same way. Many youth sports officials to whom I speak regard parent abuse as the most stressful and negative aspect of the volunteer work they do. Most of them can recount at least one incident of a parent getting out of control and attacking them verbally and, sometimes, physically. Such situations are an ugly accompaniment to youth sports contests, even though it is easy to understand how a parent with poor emotional control skills can fall prey to the strong emotions generated by children's sports.

Parents who can somehow resist the urge to criticize a bad call, who can even compliment the officials for their hard work after a game (especially if their child's team loses), are rewarded with the pleasure of seeing a surprised smile on the face of the referee or umpire. Youth sports officials tell me that such positive feedback, rare as it is, goes a long way toward motivating them to stick with their volunteer work. It keeps them going through the bad times.

Talk to Parents of the Other Team

Last year I happened to attend a state championship baseball playoff game for boys under eleven. The winner would play in the league's state final. After seven innings the game was tied and moved into extra innings. The tension in the stands among the parents I was sitting with kept rising as each extra inning passed. Mothers would cover their eyes as their son came to the plate, or hold hands tightly with the parents next to them. Finally, after ten innings one team broke through and scored the decisive run. There was more relief than jubilation from the parents of the winning team, but the parents of the other team sat in silence. Then one of the parents of the team that won went over to the parents of the other team and began shaking their hands, telling them what an exceptional and competitive game their sons had played. I watched closely and noticed the smiles on the faces of these parents, saw their shoulders lift and their energy return at this simple gesture from a member of "the opposition."

It is actions such as this from parents that give me hope that we can learn ways to overcome the behavioral excesses associated with youth sports today.

Transform the Urge to Critique

Heather, a twelve-year-old gymnast, sits in my office with tears rolling down her face. She is telling me about her father's reaction to her most recent competitive performance at a gymnastics meet in Pennsylvania. On the four-hour drive home, her father, Dennis, went over her routine with her step-by-step and listed all the errors she made. He wasn't angry, he didn't yell. He just wanted her to know how she could improve.

Of course, the problem is that Heather knew each and every error her father pointed out and also recognized some missteps and faults that he missed. She didn't need him to point out the obvious to her. But Dennis mistook her quiet stoicism in the face of a poor performance for a lack of caring. On the contrary, Heather cared a great deal about gymnastics and hated to do poorly at important meets. The resulting miscommunications between father and daughter led to a simmering conflict between them, one that Dennis was at a loss to understand.

My counseling with this family focused on two areas. First, I helped Heather to become more open with her father about the emotional impact of his criticisms of her performance. This feedback was a surprise to Dennis and helped him to tone down the stridency of his critiques. Second, I helped Dennis to explore other ways of expressing his support for Heather other than detailing her short-comings. This proved difficult for Dennis. Pointing out the mistakes of others was an approach he had grown up with in his own family, and change was hard.

At first the only way Dennis could overcome his natural ten-dencies was to remain silent. If he spoke up after a contest, he nat-urally launched into criticism. Gradually he learned to focus on the positive and was able to compliment Heather on various aspects of her routines. With the support of his wife, Dennis eventually learned that he was able to leave behind his daughter's performance com-pletely and discuss the social aspects of the experience with her. These social experiences and friendships were what Heather wanted to talk about with her parents after a tough competition. She needed time away from her performance in order to put it in perspective.

The urge to critique a child's performance is very natural for par-ents. Yet many of the successful athletes I work with remark on their parents' *lack* of criticism of their sporting performance. "They just wanted me to play and have fun" is a typical comment from an Olympic basketball player. "Mom and Dad never had much say in how I played. They left that to the coach. But I knew they were al-ways there for me, no matter how I did."

These are some of the behaviors I have observed that seem to re-duce the negative aspects of the parent trap. These parents swim against the tide. Instead of behaving in the expected way, they be-have in ways unexpected and surprising. The results? More fun at the games, more friendships among other parents, and respect from coaches and officials associated with the sport.

My experiences with youth sports over the past decade suggest to me that all parents will feel the pull of the parent trap. It's impossible to support children and put in the effort to help them succeed and then not feel strongly about how they do. But I have also observed that some parents can escape from this emotional whirlpool by looking outward, beyond their own family, and recognizing that in helping others they also end up helping themselves.

In the next chapter I examine the experiences of families when they become involved in youth sports. There are typical experiences shared by many families as their children progress from young novices to experienced adolescent athletes. Striking a balance for the entire family during this process of development is crucial for successfully negotiating the youth sports experience.

6

THE FAMILY'S JOURNEY
Nurturing Safe and Healthy Young Athletes

The centrality of sports in American life positions it to have a unique influence on families. As the previous chapters have indicated, it is natural for parents in the United States to be strongly attracted to youth sports programs and to want to place their children in them. Youth sports have become a common and central feature for the American family.

In the previous chapter I examined how the process of identification can trap parents into acting in ways that are selfish and hurtful. Sports can lure parents to behave in ways that seem almost crazy. In this chapter I reverse the equation and look at how families can proactively support a young athlete's development.

The stories of Olympic and professional athletes who have dedicated years to achieving their goals are well known, but for every athlete that is ultimately successful there are another fifty or hundred who made similar sacrifices but achieved little success. And beyond these, there are many more young people who spent several years intensively involved in sports but ended up dropping out or taking up some new activity. The question naturally arises, Is it worth it? Are the sacrifices made to help talented young athletes develop worthwhile? What impact does this intense sporting involvement have on families? And are there better ways to nurture young athletes than the typical examples held up as role models?

IN SEARCH OF EXCELLENCE

Researchers have carefully studied the families of young people who display excellence at an early age. These families, including the families of exceptional young athletes, share several defining characteristics.

Belief in the Value of Hard Work and Achievement

The research that Othon Kesend and I conducted at the Olympic Training Center underlined the fact that athletic success is a *family* affair. Both fathers and mothers received a great deal of credit from the Olympians we interviewed for introducing the young athletes to sport, for supporting their active involvement, and for providing emotional sustenance along the way. One of the basketball players we interviewed is typical. "My Mom signed me up to start playing basketball. I think another mother told her about it and said it was good for kids and she put all three of us in a program. Everything was made available to me as I got better. I never had to fight about getting a ride to the gym or anything. Whatever I needed . . . if I said, 'Dad, I need a new pair of basketball shoes,' it was, 'Here's the money, go get yourself a pair.' That sort of thing."

The families of successful young athletes tend to believe in the value of individual achievements, and they believe that hard work is the key to success. The factor that appears to trigger a family's intense commitment to the young athlete's success is the discovery that the child is talented in that sport. One of the athletes we interviewed remembers, "I was in high school and the first year I was playing on the junior varsity team, and my coach took me aside and told me I might be really good at this. And I didn't know but he told my parents that I might have a shot at the Olympic team one day. And after that things were different; my parents couldn't do enough for me. They got me extra coaching and during the summers they put me in special wrestling programs. They started watching what I ate and put me on a diet. I guess it got pretty intense."

The successful child athlete runs the risk of having the label *talented* applied to him or her. I have come to think that there is nothing as dangerous to the emotional equilibrium of a parent than having a talented youngster! The emotional pulls on the parent of a talented athlete become much stronger.

The Development of Talent

It is a fact of American life that the development of talent is one of the central themes of our society. More than people from any other country in the world, Americans value talent and its full development. There are few more hurtful appellations to apply to someone than that they are "a wasted talent." It is part of the American dream that people in this country should be able to develop their unique talents to the fullest.

In part this value is due to our competitive capitalist view of the world. Without talent development, without competition to see who can develop, produce, market, and distribute a product better than anyone else, capitalism fails. There is no hope for our capitalist philosophy in a noncompetitive environment. The importance of talent is also due to the strong individualistic, "pioneering" spirit of this country. The simplest outlook on American life suggests that we enjoy our childhood, identify our unique talents, put them to good use, lead a full and productive life, and make a contribution to society.

It is not this way in every country. As one who grew up and reached adulthood in Australia, for example, I came to realize that the Australian way of life often encourages "getting along" and not standing out from the crowd, rather than fiercely promoting the individual's right to succeed. I suspect from my travels that this is a common point of view in many countries. Certainly in no other country in the world are the rights of the individual over those of the group protected as strongly as they are in the United States. These rights are deeply embedded in the American world view.

The result is that U.S. families feel almost obligated to nurture outstanding talent once it is identified. Parents feel guilty if they do not make sacrifices to support a talented child to the fullest—and athletic talent is usually easy to identify. "Natural" athletes run faster, jump farther, and seem more coordinated than their less-talented brethren. There is a widespread expectation that parents who have a child who displays a knack for basketball or swimming or some other sport will make extra efforts to help the child progress in that sport.

Belief in the Value of Sports

Those families that do pursue a child's talent development share another defining characteristic: they value sports.

If athletic talent is to be nurtured and developed within a family, the family must value sports. As we have seen, this is a natural tendency in a society that places great emphasis on sporting prowess. Some families, however, do not value the sporting lifestyle. Sometimes this is because the parents are not athletic themselves and do not care about sports. Sometimes it is because one of the parents was an athlete and wishes to protect the child from the hardships he or she faced. In other cases, there is a perceived conflict between the value of specialization in sports and the value of other life experiences, especially education. Some families discourage a child's participation in sports in order to encourage a focus on academics.

But in families in which athletic talent is nurtured, sporting excellence is seen as valuable. Often, sports are valued because of the lessons they impart to the young person. Parents believe in the importance of working hard to reach one's goals, and the sports experience is seen as a vehicle for teaching this philosophy. Increasingly, some parents see sports participation as valuable because of the benefits it may offer the child in the future.

While some parents value sports more highly than other activities, this is not always the case for the child. Drew Pierno sits uncomfortably between his father, Tony, and his mother, Julia. His parents do most of the talking in our first meeting. At ten years of age, Drew is already playing four different sports during the year. He participates in baseball, soccer, swimming, and tennis. "But it's in tennis that he has natural talent," explains Tony. "His coach tells me that he can be a real star. But he just doesn't want to practice. He keeps saying he wants to play in the school band. I've told him no over and over again, but he doesn't seem to listen. He's wasting his talent." Tony looks at his son with exasperation, and then back to me with an imploring look. "What's wrong with him?" asks Tony plaintively. If Tony and Julia persist in forcing Drew to play sports and ignore his musical interests, problems surely lie ahead.

Sometimes parents signal to their children their belief in the value of sports in indirect ways. As Jay Coakley has pointed out, if parents *tell* their ten-year-old son that academics are more important than basketball, then skip all their son's parent-teacher meetings but show up at every basketball game, the child will soon realize that despite what his parents say, they clearly care more about basketball than about school.

Willingness to Make Sacrifices for the Talented Athlete

The final characteristic of families that successfully nurture a talented young athlete is that they are prepared to make sacrifices for the good of the child's sporting development. The family of the youth sports star organizes itself around the sporting lifestyle of the young athlete. This characteristic can be witnessed in any community on any weekend, when parents take time out of their lives to drive or accompany their children to a variety of sports contests. As I described earlier in the book, some families go to the length of splitting up in order to further the child's sports career. The father, for example, might stay in Detroit at his job and with his other three children while the mother moves to Colorado Springs with her daughter so that the young athlete might train with one of the top figure skating coaches in the country. Between these extremes lie a multitude of behaviors that illustrate the notion that families will make a variety of sacrifices to help their children become better and more successful athletes.

One of the consequences for a family that has a talented child athlete is that the *emotional* investment in the child's sports development is greater than usual. The parents value highly their child's participation in sports, so the sport experience becomes endowed with a number of emotional connotations. And the more sacrifices the family makes on behalf of the young athlete, the greater is the emotional intensity associated with the desire to see the child succeed. When sacrifices have been made for a long-term goal, and when roadblocks impede progress toward it, it is natural for strong feelings of frustration to occur.

ARE THE SACRIFICES WORTH IT?

When an elite athlete retires from sports and looks back on her career, does she typically find it all worthwhile, or does she regret the sacrifices she made? The answers are mixed. For example, sport psychologist Tara Scanlan and her colleagues from the University of California, Los Angeles, interviewed twenty-six former elite figure skaters and found that on the whole they were very satisfied with the results of their high-level sporting involvement. One skater summarized her feelings by saying, "I know how hard my parents were working and how expensive the sport was. [It was important] to know that it was all worth it at the time that I performed well. Because I saw the enjoyment in their faces and I just knew it was all worth it at that point. And that they knew it was all worth it at that point for all the hard work they had to do."

Other researchers, however, have found that some athletes end their careers on a very negative note and continue to look back on their years in sports with bitterness. Not surprisingly, if athletes are not successful, or if their long-terms goals are thwarted by injury or by lack of success, they are more likely to question the value of their athletic experience. One of my clients, Jeff, looking back at his son's ten-year career in youth swimming, summarized his feelings by saying, "It just wasn't worth it. At the time we couldn't see that; we put up with the injuries and the overtraining problems, and we gladly spent the money. But at the end, when Kevin said that he wished he had never started swimming, I felt like a total failure. I cried. I wish I could go back and do it over again."

Even highly successful athletes sometimes look back and wonder "What if?" What if they had not pursued success so single-mindedly and had led a more "normal" life? I have found that there is a high level of ambivalence about the value of a sports career, even among successful athletes. For example, in the research study conducted by Othon Kesend and me at the Olympic Training Center, one of the questions we asked the athletes was, "If you had a five-year-old child, what would you do in their upbringing, related to sports, the same or differently from your own upbringing?" More than half the athletes said that they would make sure that their child participated in other activities besides sports. Clearly the message from these athletes is that there is more to life than just sports, and they want their children to understand this.

Perhaps the key to whether a youth sports experience is considered worthwhile, in retrospect, is whether it helped the young athlete develop as a person, not just as an athlete. When parents become overidentifed and overinvested in their child, the experience is likely to be a failure. But if the family can help the child develop as an individual and grow toward maturity and independence, the youth sports experience will have done far more than teach a child a sporting skill.

NURTURING SUCCESSFUL PEOPLE, NOT JUST SUCCESSFUL ATHLETES

Psychologist Steve Danish, who has developed many programs aimed at helping children through sports, defines successful development as helping a child become personally competent. The three essential features of personal competence are the abilities to do life planning, to be self-reliant, and to seek the resources of others when needed. This is an excellent formula for avoiding the parent trap I discussed in the previous chapter. Teaching a child to be self-reliant and to do their own planning and set their own goals guarantees that parents will not make the mistake of forcing their own agenda on the child.

The issue of personal competence is, I believe, critical to the healthy development of the young athlete. The successful and happy athletes I see in my work feel supported and encouraged by their families. They have a sense of their own identity outside the family, yet they are nurtured by their family's support. The unhappy and conflicted athletes feel controlled and pressured by outside expectations. They are not pursuing their own goals but are trying to live up to the expectations of their parents.

How can families successfully negotiate the issue of supporting a child's athletic dreams and goals and allowing him or her to grow up with a sense of controlling their own destiny? The next section provides a model for this process.

SUCCESSFUL DEVELOPMENT FOR THE YOUNG ATHLETE: GUIDELINES FOR PARENTS

An interesting and useful way of thinking about the development of the young athlete has been proposed by Jon Hellstedt. He has looked at the development of the young athlete as an issue for the entire family. Not only does the young athlete go through many changes as she grows up and matures, like moving from T-ball to Little League to high school baseball, but the family also experiences many changes over the same time span. Hellstedt has made a valuable insight with this point of view. It is impossible to look at the development of the young athlete without also taking into account the changes experienced by the parents and siblings.

In the model Hellstedt has developed, he describes three main stages of development for the typical athletic family. In each stage, he has identified certain critical goals the family must achieve for successful development to occur. I have expanded on his model by examining these three stages as they relate both to the talented child athlete and to the majority of children. Many of the challenges facing a very talented and serious young athlete are different than those facing most children who participate in sports.

We need to design youth sports programs that meet the needs of both the talented minority who expect to have a long-term career in sports and the majority for whom sports is a gateway to a life-long commitment to being physically active and healthy. In both cases, helping the child to mature into an independent and self-reliant individual is crucial. Only then will the young person have the coping skills necessary to meet any challenge he may encounter.

Phase 1: Exploration

Hellstedt argues that this important stage of the athletic family's development occurs while children are between the ages of four and twelve. He does not give names to each stage in his model, but I have chosen the term *exploration phase* for this stage because it nicely emphasizes the sense of trying different sports and the excitement of exploring one's skills, which are characteristic of this stage. Of course, these ages are only guides to help us understand how a young athlete develops. In some sports, such as women's gymnastics, children tend to be very young when they get competitively involved. In other sports, such as cross-country skiing, it is my experience that athletes are usually much older when introduced to the competitive level. Sometimes a young athlete may experience several cycles of development in different sports. For example, he may begin playing soccer at age five, take up tennis at age seven, and begin running track at age thirteen.

Hellstedt points out that the family must negotiate several objectives within each phase in order for the young athlete to develop successfully and move to the next phase. For developmental progress to occur, the objectives of the parents in the exploration phase are to introduce the child to a variety of sports, to emphasize fun and skill development and minimize competitive success, and to ensure good coaching for continued participation and skill development.

The Talented Child in the Exploration Phase

The first step in talent development is obvious but often overlooked. To help a child develop her athletic talents, those talents must first be identified. Unfortunately for many gifted youngsters, many parents introduce their children only to sports they are familiar with from television. Often a talented athlete who is fairly good at a popular sport, such as basketball, could be very good in a different sport, such as wrestling or cycling. Without the opportunity to try different sports, such talents go unnoticed.

Parents sometimes think that the best way for a good young athlete to progress is to introduce him to competition as soon as possible. Far from it. One way in which competition can hinder talent development is that in higher-level competitive leagues children often have to sit on the bench to allow other children to play. The child cannot learn and develop from sitting on the bench and would be better served by participating in activities that keep the child involved.

Good coaching is clearly important for the development of athletic skills. The obvious reason is that good coaches teach children how to perform a skill well. This is what children are seeking from sports—the opportunity to learn new skills. But perhaps even more important, as sport psychologists such as Ron Smith and Frank Smoll have found, the better coaches help keep children interested in a sport. Children are more likely to keep playing for good coaches. There is no chance for a gifted athlete to develop her talents if she drops out of a sport. Good coaches promote talent development by promoting continued participation.

Promoting Participation in the Exploration Phase

Researchers have not been able to show that early childhood involvement in youth sports promotes a healthy and active adult lifestyle. But I know from experience with many clients that the reverse is definitely true: bad experiences with sports at an early age can turn an individual away from sports involvement forever. The two main culprits leading to bad experiences for children are over-emphasis on competition and bad coaching.

The same fundamentals that promote talent development in the early years also serve very well to promote participation. A diversity of sporting experiences paves the way for young people to find some activities that they will enjoy throughout life. An emphasis on fun and enjoyment keeps children involved and active. And good coaching promotes continued participation.

There is no doubt that a parent can guide a child's choices at this stage. Without the parent's involvement, what nine-year-old could sustain active sporting involvement? But the critical mistake made by parents when a child is young is to focus on their own expectations for the child and to ignore the dreams of the child. I think of the major goal of the exploration phase as nourishing the dreams of the child. Unfortunately, parents' own dreams can blind them to their child's hopes and goals, as we saw with the Morrow family in Chapter Five. Jay Morrow wanted his daughter to succeed because his goal was for Susan to get a full scholarship to a prestigious university. His ambition was for Susan—and her success would make him happy. But the trouble is that Jay's focus on his own goal led him to ignore Susan's dreams. Her ambitions were different from those of her father, and the clash between these goals caused the family problems I saw.

The solution is easy to state and difficult to accomplish. Whatever hopes the parent has for a child, it is critical to nurture the child's own dreams and ambitions, and to communicate with the child so that these dreams can be supported.

Phase 2: Commitment

The essential feature of this phase is the increasing commitment of the young athlete to her chosen sport. Hellstedt maintains that the family with adolescent children involved in sports faces several common issues. As I have observed many times in my counseling work, and as Hellstedt's model emphasizes, the major issue is the extent of the commitment on the part of the family to the young athlete's pursuits. The involvement takes the form of spending time on the sport—spending money on equipment; devoting time to practice, coaching, and travel; providing emotional support and encouragement; and organizing family activities to give priority to the child's sport.

The Talented Child in the Commitment Phase

Hellstedt's model focuses on families of talented athletes, and he identifies some of the major goals needed for such a family to develop through the commitment phase:

- Encourage and support the child's commitment to sports

- Provide emotional support to the athlete

- Provide financial support and give time to the sports activities

- Encourage the young athlete's increased independence in decision making

- Allow for a shift in influence on the young athlete from the parents to teachers and coaches

A recurring theme in most of these goals is the emphasis on the young athlete's learning to take responsibility for the talent development process. The athlete must commit to the training required to improve, must learn to make decisions independently, and must develop new relationships with coaches. As the family struggles to adjust to a member's increasing independence, conflict often occurs. Once again, the issue of supporting a young athlete's goals versus imposing expectations on him or her is critical to the successful development of the athlete.

My experience has taught me that families usually struggle with this process. Parents must believe in the goals of their child. It is difficult for parents to spend a lot of time and money on a young athlete's dreams if the parents don't share the vision.

Conflict or Burnout?

Two common problems in this stage of the family's development are excessive conflict and burnout. Many athletes I have counseled over the years have been in situations similar to Susan Morrow's experience. I vividly remember Kimberly, a fifteen-year-old figure skater, one of the top skaters in the country, sobbing in my office in Colorado Springs. "It's no fun any more," she commented bitterly. "I hate practice sessions, I hate the competitions. But how can I tell my parents? They have spent $50,000 on me in the past two years to be a successful skater. How can I let them down?" With all such athletes, one of my chief goals is to help them rediscover their own *personal* reasons for participating. If the athlete continues to participate for someone else's reasons, they are doomed to failure.

In my consulting work with coaches, teams, schools, and families, this is one of the most common problems I see. Parents, and sometimes coaches, have a different set of expectations or goals than the young athlete. Naturally this often leads to conflict. But it is only the strongest and most confident children who have the skills to resist the expectations of their parents and to fight for their own dreams. In some ways, when I see a family in open conflict, such as the Morrows were, I am relieved, because it makes my job easier. The family has already identified the problem and is struggling, sometimes ineffectively, to solve it.

More insidious, and more difficult to deal with, is the more common case where the child gives up on her own dreams and adopts the goals of her parents or coach. When the athlete adopts others' goals for herself, it often leads to burnout.

The reason for this is simple, yet the implications are complex. We do things because we enjoy them. Have you ever tried to get someone to exercise who didn't like exercise? I have, and I know it's a tough assignment. In fact, I have slowly realized that it is impossible (at least for me). But have you ever tried to get a runner who loves running to stop? You can't. They won't let you.

If we enjoy something, it has such intrinsic, personal value for us that we will move mountains to have the chance to do it. Whether it be music, art, sports, our work, or our relationships, we are committed to the things we enjoy. And this enjoyment is a personal experience. It is intensely subjective. In fact, the thing I enjoy might be something you actively dislike.

This enjoyment is important because every survey and study of young athletes finds that the number one reason that young athletes play sports is because they are fun. Yet so many older athletes I work with are not having fun anymore. What happened to them?

Losing the Love of the Game: Externalization

I have come to realize that a crucial change in perspective occurs when sports stop being what the young athlete does for intrinsic pleasure and become something he does for a reason. The young athlete doesn't need a reason to play basketball—he loves it. There is nothing he would rather do than dribble around and shoot at the hoop. But when his practice sessions are for a reason—to get a scholarship, to win a game, to impress a scout, to please his father—suddenly some of the fun is gone. As long as the intrinsic drive to play predominates, the athlete is OK. But when the external reasons for playing take over, the game becomes a chore, and burnout becomes likely.

We might call this process the *externalization* of sports. Clearly it is promoted in children by parents such as Jay Morrow, who push their own goals and expectations onto their child's sports participation. But as the young athlete moves through the commitment phase, sports are often externalized by coaches and institutions. Coaches begin to tell very talented players that they might be good enough to get a scholarship or make it to the pros, schools begin to reward their winning athletes with special events or award banquets, and competitive events are structured so that the best athletes and teams get the opportunity to travel to national competitions or to play interstate rivals. At every step, externalization becomes a problem for the most talented and hard-working athletes. The problem is that the external reasons for playing sports begin to outnumber the internal, personal reasons.

Whether the pressure to participate for external reasons becomes stressful for the athlete seems to depend on how much control the athlete feels he has over the situation. If he still feels in control, if his athletic participation is part of his self-development, then sports can be a healthy part of the process of growing up. If the athlete feels controlled, however, and feels that he is not making the decisions or developing as in individual, then burnout is more likely.

Coakley interviewed fifteen adolescent athletes who had been age-group champions in their sport but had then quit. He found that the way high-level sports were organized contributed to the decision to quit for these young athletes. They felt little control over their own lives, a situation made worse because they had made such a commitment to the sport that the sport almost *was* their whole life. They felt they had little identity outside that of being an athlete. This lack of control and restricted identity caused a great deal of stress, and the sport ceased to be fun. At some stage, despite the potential for continued success, the athlete made the decision to quit.

Recently I was discussing the issue of burnout with a professional hockey player. A graduate of the youth ice hockey leagues, as were most of his teammates, Pat told me that a great many talented players never make it to the highest levels of ice hockey. "I feel bad for kids who are victims of their parents' competitiveness," said Pat. "I used to play with a kid, Justin, who was always more talented than I. But his father was a terror. Once, the under-eleven team that the father was coaching lost the league championship game when little Justin didn't score a goal in the overtime shoot-out. His father threw his equipment out of the car as they were driving down the highway after the game. I went on to play with this kid in college and he never seemed to enjoy the game. His dad still came to all the games and you knew he was in the building because you could hear him scream at his son from the stands."

"Justin was a great player," Pat continued. "He probably would have gone on to the pros, but he couldn't tell his dad to back off and it ended up making him compete for all the wrong reasons. Justin wasn't competitive like that. It took the fun out of the game for him."

Pat's example highlights the dilemma for the adolescent athlete in the commitment phase whose parents are not supportive of the child's goals and instead impose their own goals on the athlete. On the one hand, the athlete can resist this pressure from the parents, but conflict inevitably ensues. On the other hand, if the young athlete buys into the goals of the parent, they are being unfaithful to their own dreams and are likely to feel less in control of their lives. If their own ambitions and goals are not nurtured, young people can lose the valuable sense of self-determination—that they are the agents of change in their own lives. Trying to live up to someone else's expectations is not as motivating or enjoyable as pursuing your own goals, and it is not surprising that so many athletes I see placed in this situation end up terminating their sports involvement.

The Underinvolved Parent

Recently I gave a workshop for coaches to discuss the issues of burnout and conflict that I have just described. Two tennis coaches came up to me afterwards and told me they wished they had some parents who were overinvolved in their children's sports. Their problem was that parents would not support their children in tennis, wouldn't drive them to competitions, and wouldn't buy them equipment.

This is a different kind of problem than overidentification, which is the focus of this book. Some parents display no interest whatsoever in the sporting activities of their children. This causes two main problems. First, it is very difficult for the young athlete whose parents are underinvolved to become committed to a sport. This can place a great burden on the coach, who often feels for the athlete and tries to make up for the parents' lack of support. Most coaches are very caring toward their athletes and will go the extra mile for the athlete who is eager to play but who lacks support. But it is a difficult situation, and there are no easy answers for the athlete or for the coach.

Second, the few coaches who are likely to abuse a young athlete have an increased opportunity when the parents are not involved in their child's activities. That is why I encourage parents to form a good relationship with their child's coaches, and why I encourage coaches to be open to parents who want to know what goes on at practices and on trips to tournaments and so on. In this day and age it is wise to be careful about the choice of who is placed in a caretaker position with young children.

Underinvolved parents are not responsible for the crisis in youth sports today. But they do contribute to problems for young athletes. Good sports programs for children reach out to parents and encourage them in a variety of ways to become involved in the lives of the children.

Promoting Participation in the Commitment Phase

The objective for the family of the talented athlete is to support the athlete through a period of continued participation to achieve greater skill development. The same objective must be pursued if we are to encourage more young people simply to be physically active and fit, but the goals of the athletes are different. For most athletes, the dream of being the next Michael Jordan or Wayne Gretzky has faded by the time adolescence is reached. Only the most talented athletes remain focused on a career in sports, or on playing sports at a high level through the collegiate years.

But this doesn't mean that the majority of young people have no aspirations for their athletic involvement. In fact, I find that young people have a myriad of hopes and expectations regarding their involvement in sports. These goals vary enormously, from becoming good enough at a sport to play it competitively throughout life, to having enough skill to enjoy having fun playing with friends on weekends. The challenge for our society is to find ways to meet this tremendous variety of needs, and also to meet society's desperate need to promote greater physical fitness. Our society is good at meeting the needs of the talented few in sports. It has failed badly in meeting the needs of the "untalented" many.

The challenge for parents is to promote a love of healthy physical activity in their child during a time of development when there are many competing demands on a child's time. A question I am often asked is, How far should I push my son or daughter to participate in sports before I give up? I think this question shows that many parents don't know how to tap the child's intrinsic love of physical activity and play.

As I discussed in Chapter Four, there is little that is more natural than a child's love of physical activity and skill learning. The question is not how to push a child toward sports but how to enhance a child's intrinsic attraction to physical games. Unfortunately, many youth sports programs turn children off by being boring, repetitive, overly demanding, or insensitive to the needs of children. There is no need for parents to beat their heads (or the head of their child) against a brick wall when encountering such a program. There are too many good programs out there to waste time on bad ones.

Parents can certainly help children develop an intrinsic motivation to participate in sports. If the developmental steps described in this chapter are followed, children can grow up learning to make their own decisions about their sporting involvement. This is critical for the development of inner-directed motivation. Parents can help introduce children to a variety of sports experiences, they can search for good coaches who will truly help their child learn, and they can model commitment, enjoyment, and perseverance in their own physical activity. The last is very important. Children learn by observing the actions of those around them. Parents who show that they are committed to their own health and passionate about their own physical activities teach their children to be similarly committed to their own sporting involvements.

A personal anecdote might illustrate how parents can influence a child's lifelong attitude toward sports at this phase without pushing. When I was ten, like most young Australians I was a keen fan of cricket and rugby. These were the sports I watched, and the sports I played. My parents suggested that I try tennis, but I rejected the suggestion, feeling that tennis was not exciting enough for me. My parents then approached me in a more circuitous fashion. They told me that my best friend, Simon, was learning tennis, and asked me if I would go with him for some lessons. With my best friend alongside, tennis seemed a more palatable option, and I agreed. I found that I loved the game. Better yet, my younger brother also picked the game up, and we found we could play against each other for hours at a neighborhood court. Simon soon left tennis to try other pursuits. I am still playing thirty years later. In fact, I play tennis three times a week, and I often thank God that my parents got me started in such a great game. It is both a fun social activity and a good path to fitness for me. If my parents had tried to pressure me to play thirty years ago, who knows what the outcome might have been?

There is no easy answer for the parent attempting to guide a child through this stage of development. Of course the parent will have hopes and aspirations for the child. And it can be an emotionally wrenching experience for the caring parent to see a talented young athlete who does not develop that talent. It is natural to push the child, to try to help him succeed. But at some stage of development parents must let go of their own hopes for their child and trust the child to pursue his own goals. Even successful progress through this stage is usually fraught with struggle and pain. It is the nature of the process. But good communication helps both parents and children successfully negotiate the obstacles that can block development. If parents listen to the young athlete, they can avoid conflict caused by ignoring the goals of the child. And young athletes must communicate their ambitions and hopes to their parents if they are to avoid passive acceptance of an external set of goals—a road that usually leads to burnout.

Phase 3: Proficiency

This phase of athletic development is very different when talent development is being pursued than when the main focus is promoting participation. When an athlete is talented and strives to develop that talent to the fullest, the proficiency phase requires long hours of training, intense coaching or studying of the sport, and participation in very competitive events. The young athlete grows into a truly expert performer. But for most athletes, the proficiency phase involves becoming good enough to reach one's goals, whether that goal is playing on an intramural rugby team or being good enough to participate in a five-kilometer road race without being embarrassed.

The Talented Child in the Proficiency Phase

As the young athlete matures and takes ownership of his sporting participation, there comes a time when the athletic role becomes a central feature of the young person's life. Often this occurs as early as high school—in some sports even earlier—and in our culture it is characteristic of the life of the college athlete, particularly in the "big-time" sports. A few athletes even specialize in sports to such an extent that they make a living from them for some years, as professional or perhaps Olympic-caliber athletes.

Hellstedt proposes that the main goals for families negotiating this period of sports development are

- Allow the athlete to gain emotional and financial independence from their parents

- Provide continued emotional support and a refuge from the pressures of competition
- Accept the authority of the coach and become less prominent in the decision-making process

In the study we conducted of Olympic athletes, Kesend and I found that the emotional support factor was very important to elite athletes. The athletes told us that parents were a major source of encouragement to them in their persistent efforts to achieve success. Parents often supported their children in indirect ways, by being positive role models, by giving verbal and nonverbal approval of athletic successes, by showing emotional acceptance of decisions, and by sharing ideas with the athlete.

We also found, however, that parents had the potential to be a source of discouragement for excellent athletes. Parents who were critical of their child's efforts, who reacted negatively to continued sporting participation, and who expressed doubts about the potential for success were seen as an obstacle by the elite athletes we interviewed. When conflict arose between these athletes and their parents, it was usually over disagreements about the goals of the athlete, or over perceived lack of support. Despite such conflict, these Olympic athletes had persisted. No doubt many others exposed to similar negativity decide not to go on.

If we look at this situation from a parent's point of view, we can see the dilemma they face. It is easier to support a talented athlete when success is frequent. The success makes all the sacrifices worthwhile. It is much harder to support the young athlete in the face of frequent setbacks and disappointments. Often parents feel that perhaps they should be the one to provide a "dose of reality" to the struggling athlete. After all, the very nature of sports is such that success is reserved for the few. Most athletes will experience failure more often than success. This is the nature of competition. But a struggling athlete often does not want to think about the potential disappointments of continued participation.

The solution, once again, is to focus on the young athlete's intrinsic motivation. The final decision about whether to continue must be made by the athlete himself. Parents and coaches can provide input, but they do not have to live out the decision every day as the athlete does. Only an athlete who plays with an inner desire to keep improving, to keep pushing on, will have the emotional resources to handle the inevitable setbacks along the way.

Maintaining this inner fire becomes, paradoxically, more difficult as athletes experience greater levels of success. For collegiate and professional athletes, the move away from participating in sports for intrinsic reasons to playing sports solely for external reasons is often complete. As we hear so often from athletes today, sports is a career. For a very few it is a lucrative career. For most it represents the opportunity to live a marginal economic existence doing something they are very good at and that they once—perhaps even still—loved doing. Collegiate athletes do not receive direct financial compensation but are rewarded either with scholarships that pay for tuition and board or by the recognition and perks that come with being a collegiate athlete. For most of them, at least in the well-known sports, the end of their collegiate athletic career is also the end of the sporting road.

The result is that many top-level athletes end up playing out careers for largely external reasons and have stopped enjoying what they once did for the intrinsic reasons that initially motivated them. This externalization is, I believe, a factor contributing to many of the behavior problems we see today among top-level athletes. Drug abuse, alcoholism, marital conflicts, sexual transgressions, and violence are sometimes the symptoms of unhappy people who feel a fundamental disconnection between what they do and who they are. Athletes must be able to develop a sense of self-confidence beyond the confidence they derive solely from their sports performance. Otherwise, the athlete's confidence always depends on her most recent performance. No amount of money, I have found, can cure this problem. The only cure, just as for young athletes, is finding a way to recapture one's personal dreams and ambitions. The athletes who do this, who maintain that inner desire, are a joy to watch. Even the novice sports fan can soon tell the difference between the two.

Promoting Participation in the Proficiency Phase

As they mature into adulthood, most people have athletic or sports-related goals that revolve around fitness, health, and enjoyment issues. There is no need to become an expert performer to reach such goals. But this stage of sporting involvement is the most important for our society as a whole. Here is where we lose participants in massive numbers. As adults, two-thirds of us are sedentary, with disastrous health-related consequences. This is the most poorly understood phase of the sports development process.

Consequently, to me the proficiency phase is the most interesting aspect of our participation in sports. How do youngsters grow up with a lifelong love of sports and a commitment to sustained participation in physical activity? How can the majority of people be encouraged to continue their athletic activity over the adult life span? As adults, we don't need to be expert performers, but we do need to be able to stay active, fit, healthy, and energized. What impact does a child's experience in youth sports have on her adult sports or exercise involvement? Are the adult's attitudes toward physical activity shaped on the playing fields of childhood? Are bad sports experiences as a child related to lack of involvement in adult sporting activities? Do good experiences promote a lifelong commitment to fitness and good health?

We don't have answers to these questions, but I believe the evidence we have examined already strongly suggests that our sports programs fail us when we need them most. Instead of promoting mass participation, we focus on a talented few (often failing them as well) and ignore the needs of the rest. Overly competitive youth sports programs turn young people away from sports in huge numbers. Restrictive resources and facilities limit opportunities to participate.

We end up promoting a sedentary society because we organize our youth sports and adult programs in this way. Children will stop dropping out of youth sports programs if the programs meet their needs. If adults stop organizing these programs on the basis of their own motives, great changes are possible. Perhaps such changes can also begin to permeate our high schools and colleges. Can you imagine what such institutions might be like if sports programs were developed for *all* students, not just for an elite few who provide entertainment for the rest?

NURTURING THE YOUNG ATHLETE

The following list highlights my recommendations for parents based upon the developmental perspective presented in this chapter. It is helpful for parents to be clear about their own goals for youth sport involvement and to realize that these goals must be flexible in order to adapt to the child's development.

Guidelines for Parents of Young Athletes

In the exploration phase:

- There are many sport and physical activity possibilities beyond the traditional sports. Now is a good time to build a life-long commitment to an active lifestyle. Consider a variety of choices for children.

- Children are not emotionally and cognitively ready to compete at this age. Minimize competitive experiences and work on building a mastery focus toward activities (see Chapter Seven). Look for programs that support this philosophy.

- Encourage intrinsic motivation from an early age. Will your child continue to be fit and active as an adult?

- Communicate with your child's coaches. Be involved and be proactive in finding good coaches who share your values.

In the commitment phase:
- Encourage your child's interest in physical activities.

- As your child deals with competition, be there with emotional support. Focus on helping your child learn valuable life skills.

- Encourage your child to be involved in the decision making regarding sport choices. This is the age for the child to learn to be self-reliant.

- When decisions have been made with your input, reinforce and support your child's decisions and commitment. This is the time to learn about perseverance, commitment, and delay of gratification.

- Realize that a shift in influence is likely as your child looks to peers, teachers, and coaches for guidance. Keep building good communication with coaches and teach your child to do likewise.

In the proficiency phase:
- The goal for a healthy young adult is personal competence. Support the emotional and financial independence of your child.

- You will always be the parent. You can always supply emotional support and a refuge from the pressures of competition.

- Coaches are the best source of criticism for the young athlete. Focus on parenting rather than coaching. An effective parent sets limits and expectations.

ALTERNATIVE PATHS

I find the developmental perspective I have shared here to be extremely useful to parents struggling to navigate the often complex road of youth sports participation. This perspective emphasizes that young athletes will often have very different goals for the same activity, depending on their talent level and their level of development, and that is OK. Yet across all the stages, some fundamental principles apply. The most basic is the notion that the young individual must be supported to assume responsibility gradually for making her own decisions and setting her own goals. If parents, coaches, or administrators impose their own goals and ignore what the young athlete wants, problems are sure to follow. Responsibility must be taught and modeled during the exploration phase, encouraged during the commitment phase, and supported during the proficiency phase.

Finally, adopting a developmental perspective does not mean that all families or all individuals need to develop in the same manner to be successful. Organized youth sports experiences are not necessary either for developing talent or for promoting participation. They are merely the most common means of achieving these two goals. For example, golfer Greg Norman, rated the number one golfer in the world for nearly a decade, began playing golf when he was sixteen. The fact that he did not play golf during his childhood and early adolescence did not hurt the development of his phenomenal talent.

Recently I met a forty-seven-year-old woman who had taken up ice hockey five years before. Although she did not play the sport as a child—in fact, she had not engaged in any organized youth sports programs—she has been able to find a sporting activity she can enjoy as an adult. We spoke for half an hour and she described her commitment to her new sport with great passion. Ice hockey helps her maintain her fitness, and she finds that it gives her a high energy level.

The moral of these two examples is that even if children are not involved in sports programs while they are young, the development of talent and the promotion of high levels of sports participation can still occur. Youth sports programs are the most important vehicle for achieving these two goals, but they are not the only vehicle.

A major theme of the progression from exploration to commitment to proficiency in sporting development is the increasing emphasis on competition. Some children seem to adapt naturally to competitive situations, while others always seem to find competition a struggle. Competition is so omnipresent in our society that having the skills to manage one's performance successfully in competitive situations can be a huge advantage. Children learn the skills needed to be successful competitors at an early age, and many of the important lessons they learn are found in sports. But many parents and kids discover a distinct dark side to competition in youth sports, the topic of the next two chapters.

HOW CHILDREN BECOME COMPETITIVE

Many concerned adults fear that the basic reason for the growing crisis in youth sports is that these sports have become too competitive. A twelve-year-old child can be faced with a bewildering array of choices of where to play, from recreational and town leagues to "traveling" and "select" teams, and to statewide and national underage competitions. Clearly many parents get caught up in the race for their child to be the best, to win a league, a state title, a national championship. Critics argue that children exposed to such programs are likely to become overly competitive themselves.

What does it mean if a child is *competitive?* It is an emotionally charged word, carrying different meanings for different people. A father calls me on the phone and tells me that his tennis-playing daughter is "not competitive enough." He wants her to develop the "killer instinct" so that she can close out tough matches. A fifteen-year-old basketball player is working with me because, in his words, "I'm just way too competitive out on the court. A call goes against me, or we miss an easy shot, and I just lose control." His goal is to become less competitive. Recently I was discussing the topic of excellence with the superintendent of a school district and he commented that his goal is for the district to "become very competitive with the best school systems. We need to help our children compete for excellence, in sports and in academics." But when I talked to one of the teachers in his schools, she observed that in the classroom she "doesn't like to see the children be too competitive, not like they are in sports."

If children are competitive, is that good or bad? Is the competitive nature of our youth sports programs the reason for the crisis in youth sports? And how do children become competitive in the first place?

COMPETITIVE ORIENTATION

Parents are right to be concerned about what youth sports competitions teach their children, for competitions are powerful learning experiences. In fact, there are many who fiercely champion the benefits of exposing children to competitive sports as a way of preparing them for life and teaching them valuable skills such as teamwork and leadership. But others are just as vehement in their criticism of youth sports competitions as destructive learning experiences that tear down self-esteem. In fact, both sides are wrong. Youth sports competitions are not, by their nature, either character-building or harmful. It is the way we organize and structure these competitions that has the greatest influence on children. A child can have a wonderful, confidence-building experience in youth sports, or a miserable, ego-deflating experience. It depends on how adults organize the experience. My hope is that adults will try to structure youth sports programs so that they deliver the maximum benefit to all children.

Whether competition is confidence building or ego deflating depends largely on the attitude of the athlete. Sport psychology researchers have found that by the time they reach adolescence, young people have developed a stable set of attitudes toward competition. One of the most important aspects of this attitude is what psychologists call goal orientation, or what we might call *competitive orientation*. This attitude explains what an athlete focuses on in competition, how athletes will behave in different competitive situations, and what sorts of goals they are likely to set in competition.

There are two main dimensions of an athlete's competitive orientation. They are called ego orientation and mastery orientation.

Ego Orientation   *why competitive*

The athlete with an ego orientation toward competition wants to look good. The most important question for such an athlete is, How do I compare with others? One might say that athletes with this approach want to protect their egos by always appearing to be successful, to be winners. Naturally the result of competition is very important to such athletes. They want to win and do well, because it makes them look good. Losing is to be avoided at all costs, because it hurts their self-image of being a successful athlete.

Sport psychologists have found that athletes vary greatly on this dimension. Some athletes are very ego-oriented, others hardly at all. An athlete's level of ego orientation can be measured and tracked over time.

Mastery Orientation

The athlete with a mastery orientation toward competition wants to become excellent in that sport. The most important question for such an athlete is, How much have I improved my skills? One might say that athletes with this approach want to master their sport, to become experts, or at least to be as good as they can possibly be. The results of competition may be important to such athletes, but only if those results help them determine how much they have improved. Such an athlete will not be satisfied with a win if he played badly in the process.

Athletes also vary greatly in their level of mastery orientation, with some athletes possessing this attitude to a great extent while others have it very little. An important question is, Are ego and mastery orientations mutually exclusive, or can one athlete have both orientations at the same time? A number of research studies have assumed that these two orientations are at opposite ends of the same dimension. That is, if you are an ego-oriented athlete, you are not a mastery-oriented athlete. Now, however, many sport psychologists believe that both tendencies exist within us, to a greater or lesser extent.

A graphical illustration of this relationship is presented in Figure 7.1. This graphic suggests that an athlete can be high, moderate, or low on either the ego or the mastery dimension. He or she can fall into one of the four quadrants represented. The strength of an athlete's orientation on these two dimensions will have significant implications for the way the athlete deals with competitive situations. One way to think about how competitive orientation affects an athlete is to examine how athletes in each of the four quadrants are likely to behave.

High Ego, High Mastery

Stacie is an active fourteen-year-old who plays three sports. She has been playing soccer since age six, she began gymnastics at seven, and two years ago she began to play basketball. She is very competitive in her team sports and has been the captain of her age-select soccer team for two years. She loves to win and is good at encouraging her teammates if they get behind in a game. Stacie is a midfield player and is always looking to improve her skills. She goes to soccer summer camps every year to work on her game. In gymnastics she is not as talented as some of her peers, but she keeps working hard to reach higher levels in her sport. Stacie loves basketball, because it gives her a new team sport to play at school. She has a lot to learn about the game, but enjoys each step she takes.

Stacie is an example of a high ego and high mastery athlete. Such an athlete is often thought of as very competitive. She wants good results, but she also wants to develop the skills needed to excel in her sport. Competitions are a means of testing her progress against others. She likes to win contests, but if she loses she has her own internal set of standards by which to judge her performance. Her sense of her own competence in sports comes both from comparing herself to others and from comparing her progress on the relevant skills of her sport.

Figure 7.1. Orientation to Competition.

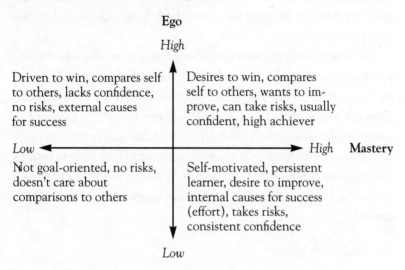

Ego

High

Driven to win, compares self to others, lacks confidence, no risks, external causes for success

Desires to win, compares self to others, wants to improve, can take risks, usually confident, high achiever

Low ◄─────────────────────────► *High*   **Mastery**

Not goal-oriented, no risks, doesn't care about comparisons to others

Self-motivated, persistent learner, desire to improve, internal causes for success (effort), takes risks, consistent confidence

Low

High Ego, Low Mastery

Dianne has been playing tennis since she was seven. She is now a freshman trying to win a spot on her high school varsity team. Her father was a college player and coached Dianne for the first five years. He understands the importance of being mentally strong in this game and he began to enter Dianne in tournaments at an early age. She progressed rapidly and is now ranked number three in New England in her age group. Dianne is a very serious player and gets very upset if she loses a match. In fact, she has recently received warnings in several tournaments for her behavior during matches—throwing her racquet and screaming loudly. She wants to become the number one player on her high school team and is looking forward to the chance to play the current team captain. But her coach has noticed that she doesn't put much effort into her practice sessions and isn't interested in doing extra workouts to help her teammates.

Dianne is an example of a high ego, low mastery athlete. Athletes in this quadrant are driven to succeed. More importantly, perhaps, they must be seen to succeed. Their frame of reference for judging their performance is the performance of others. This athlete feels more competent when she has defeated others in a contest. She does not have an internal set of standards by which she judges her own performance.

This athlete may experience problems when she encounters roadblocks or setbacks. She is likely to become frustrated if she experiences little success, because her greatest motivation is winning. This athlete is probably also most susceptible to the pressure to cheat or take shortcuts in order to succeed, because results are more important to her than how they are achieved. This athlete usually tries to avoid competitive situations in which she is likely to fail, unless she has a good excuse, such as her opponent was more highly ranked.

Low Ego, High Mastery

Michael comes from a family of wrestlers. His father, uncles, and older brothers all competed at the sport. Michael began wrestling at the age of eight and immediately liked the demands of the sport, the speed and strength required, and the need to understand your opponent and to think ahead of him at all times. Michael admired his club coach, a former national champion, and traveled extensively to wrestling meets in order to meet the best athletes in his area. By watching older wrestlers, and by asking for help from his more experienced relatives, he gained a deep understanding of the complex moves required to excel. Michael has a deep respect for his opponents. His goal is not really just to beat them, but to push himself to his limits by testing himself against them. He is probably one of the top thirteen-year-old wrestlers in the country, but he doesn't care about national rankings. His dream is to be good enough to make the USA Olympic Team. Most of the many trophies he has garnered are stored in boxes in his parents' basement. Coaches and officials who see him wrestle admire his maturity and agree that he is a great ambassador for his sport.

Michael is representative of the athlete who has a high mastery orientation and a low ego orientation. This athlete is motivated chiefly by the desire to become excellent within his chosen sport. He likes to learn new skills and is motivated when he sees improvement. He is likely to be a more persistent athlete in his pursuit of excellence, because roadblocks will be seen as a challenge to his mastery of the sport. Failures will cause less frustration to him than to other athletes, because he doesn't care about how he looks compared to others. If the athlete can see progress he will feel reinforced, even if he is losing while improving.

Coaches are sometimes puzzled by this type of athlete, because he does not fit into the image of the fiercely competitive individual typical of the high ego, high mastery athlete. Indeed, this athlete is likely to be highly self-motivated, although he will seek out good coaching in order to improve his skills.

Low Ego, Low Mastery

Sam is the running back for his Pop Warner football team. At age twelve he is already nearly six feet tall and he possesses outstanding speed. He regularly plays against children older than him, but his uncanny running ability helps him succeed no matter who he lines up against. Sam's father was an All-American in college and hopes to see Sam exceed him by making it to the pros.

Sam hates football. He's not sure if he likes any sport, but he knows he doesn't enjoy this game, playing against children older than him who regularly taunt him. When Sam asks his father if he can drop football and try something else, his dad becomes angry, so now he keeps quiet and tries to please his father. Sam's successes on the football field give him little pleasure. He never feels that he has to try very hard, and he sometimes wonders why other children seem unable to stop him. He has no goals to continue in football, and hopes that soon he can try other things, perhaps skiing and snowboarding, which he watches on TV.

The final quadrant of Figure 7.1 represents athletes like Sam who have low levels of both types of goal orientations. If this athlete is participating in a sport, it is not because he is trying to reach certain goals. His motivation most likely derives from other sources, such as a desire to be with his friends, or a need to receive attention from parents who reinforce sports participation. With neither mastery nor ego-oriented goals, however, it is unlikely that this athlete will remain in sports for very long. The challenge with such athletes is to help them find healthy activities they can enjoy, and to help them begin to set their own sporting goals.

THE EFFECTS OF COMPETITION ON COMPETITIVE ORIENTATION

In my work with many athletes, I have found that the world of sports highly reinforces the ego orientation. Think of the first questions that are usually asked of a child when she returns from a soccer match or swim meet: "How did you do?" and "Did you win?" I have seen many parents try to motivate their child by offering a tangible reward—perhaps a dollar, or a trip to the local ice cream store—for every goal they score, or for every match they win. Such efforts reinforce a child for focusing on a result rather than on a skill (though skill is needed to achieve success).

This is not a bad thing if the child also begins to learn a mastery orientation. Then the motivation to succeed will be supported by the motivation to build the skills that will fuel success. But the analysis just presented suggests that the young athlete who is highly ego oriented but has little mastery orientation is likely to run into problems in sports. He is likely to be less persistent and more easily frustrated, more likely to cheat, and perhaps more likely to quit in the face of failure than the athlete who is high in mastery orientation.

In Table 7.1, I present my thoughts about the probable consequences for the young athlete of a competitive orientation.

I believe that for athletes who have high levels of both competitive orientations, the mastery orientation tends to guide attitudes and behaviors. This will depend, however, on the relative strength of each orientation, and on the nature of the competitive situation the athlete is in. From my experience, when the stakes are very high

Table 7.1. Differences in Approach to Competition Based on the Orientation Adopted.

High Ego	High Mastery
1. Only winners profit. Losers get nothing.	1. There are multiple paths to victory. Losing brings progress and development.
2. Fear your opponents, for they might beat you. If you win, they lose.	2. Strong opponents bring greater achievement on your part. Your strength pushes others to excel.
3. The value of competition lies in the prize to be won.	3. The value of competition is personal development and long-term success.
4. Happiness comes from winning.	4. Happiness comes from becoming good at what you love.
5. Sportsmanship is peripheral to competition. Cheating is OK if you can get away with it.	5. Sportsmanship is part of the essence of competition. Cheating robs you of success.
6. If you win the prize, nothing is left for the losers.	6. Your success creates more opportunities for others.
7. Practice is useful if it makes you look good. Otherwise, avoid it.	7. Practice provides the opportunity to become good at something you enjoy.

and the perceived pressure is great, the ego orientation tends to predominate. It is often difficult for athletes in high-pressure competitive situations to focus on their mastery-oriented goals.

The concept of competitive orientation helps explain what it means to be competitive. In fact, there are several ways to approach competition. Most people would say that an athlete with a high ego orientation is very competitive. Clearly this athlete wants to win. But many would say that an athlete who is low on ego orientation is not competitive, even if such an athlete has a high mastery orientation. Yet such an athlete may still be a great competitor. In fact, over the long term, the most effective competitors usually have a high mastery orientation. The athlete most likely to experience problems in competition is the high ego, low mastery athlete.

For parents of young athletes, an important question is, How do I help my child learn to become an effective competitor? Parents know that their child will be exposed to competitive situations throughout life. They want their child to be successful in such situations. How do children learn to deal with competition? How does a young athlete's competitive orientation develop?

How Children Develop a Competitive Orientation

The most important thing to remember in discussing how children develop a competitive orientation is that many changes occur during childhood. This is a developmental issue. How a six-year-old approaches competition will be different from how a ten-year-old approaches competition, which in turn will differ from how a fifteen-year-old approaches competition. Children are not little adults, mentally or physically. This is a mistake often made by parents and by youth sports coaches. They expect children to understand competitive sports from an adult's perspective. Children, however, have their own perspective, which is sometimes difficult for adults to remember.

Sport psychologists have found that three aspects of a child's understanding of competition change significantly during development. First, children's ability to understand distinctions between effort and ability changes. Second, there are developmental changes in how good children believe themselves to be at sports. And third, as children grow older, they change the way in which they decide how good they are at sports.

Effort or Ability?

Before age nine, children have what psychologists call an *undifferentiated* concept of effort and ability. Simply put, young children make no distinction between effort and ability. A child losing a race is just as likely to explain it by saying that she didn't try hard enough as she is to say that someone is faster than her. Given another chance, the child will expect to win if she tries harder. As adults, it is hard for us to remember how the world appeared to us when we were young. It is nearly impossible for us to imagine what it feels like to see a world in which outcomes are determined solely by effort. Yet this is the world that young children inhabit.

A positive side effect of this way of seeing the world is that young children are not easily discouraged by failure. Whereas adults we might look at a series of failures and begin to question our talent, a young child might resolve simply to try harder, and will try again with high hopes. This effect is clear in the joyful enthusiasm of young children toward youth sports.

Between the ages of nine and eleven (all these ages are approximate, and will vary by individual), the concepts of effort and ability begin to differentiate. That is, children of this age begin to see it as possible that some children have more talent than others. A winning performance by another child may now be seen as indicative of a greater ability level. Children are not logical, however, about applying this insight to all situations. While an adult would now begin to use *ability* as a concept to explain all performances, a child at this age is still likely to believe that more effort will overcome any differences in ability.

The two concepts of effort and ability become fully differentiated after age eleven. Children of this age now realize that ability is a capacity, and that on any given sporting task, their own ability may be high or low. Children realize that some children are faster, stronger, and more coordinated, and have more endurance or faster reflexes than others. A consequence of this realization is that when children experience failure, they are now more likely to see it as a result of their own lack of ability. After about age eleven, participation in youth sports can begin to have a significant impact on the sporting self-confidence of a child. It is a challenge to motivate children to work to improve on skills or tasks that they don't see themselves as good at. It is interesting that children begin to leave youth sports programs in large numbers at about the same age that the concepts of ability and effort become fully differentiated. It suggests that the two may be related.

How Good Am I at Sports?

The mental development of children, as just explained, has a direct impact on their beliefs about how good they are at sports. Up until the ages of nine through eleven, children are likely to be highly optimistic about their sporting prowess. At these young ages, children simply equate sports ability with effort and they believe that their effort is under their control. The combination of a high level of sporting self-confidence with the ubiquity of sporting idols in our culture might help explain why so many children truly believe they can "be like Mike." At this age, the fantasy of one day being a superstar athlete can seem very real to children. They do not seriously question or doubt themselves, as adults do.

How Do I Know How Good I Am at Sports?

The final factor that we know shapes a child's beliefs about his or her sporting ability is the *source* of the child's judgment. As children grow, they move from depending on external sources for deciding how good they are at sports toward internal standards of reference.

When children are very young, they are highly influenced by the adults around them. If a parent or teacher tells a child, "You are very fast," the child will uncritically accept this information. At such young ages, children are also highly influenced by the fact that they can do things. For example, a child who throws a ball and hits a chosen target is likely to regard herself as good at throwing. Why? Because she hit the target. Whether the target was easy to hit or difficult is not a factor in her judgment. The simple fact of completing the throw is evidence of her throwing ability.

Only gradually do children begin to be influenced by comparisons with other children. Sport psychology researchers have found that children around age nine or ten are still highly dependent on adults for feedback as to their sporting ability. But by age twelve or thirteen, children are able to compare themselves to others. Now a young athlete will judge himself as fast only if he can beat other children his age in a race. The young athlete will no longer consider herself a good thrower just for hitting the target. If everyone else can hit the target too, she now understands that her ability is not greater than that of others. Only if she can throw more accurately than other children will her high self-confidence in her throwing ability persist.

If the young athlete continues to develop and mature, she eventually begins to form independent judgments about her sports abilities. For example, a more mature athlete will not think highly of a victory over her competitors in a race if she didn't race well. She might win, but she might be unsatisfied with her effort or her technique. Now she has developed an internal set of criteria by which she judges herself and her performance. The maturity to develop such internal criteria marks the passage to a mastery orientation toward competition. Some young athletes never develop this ability to judge themselves independently, and they remain in an ego orientation toward their sporting ability.

DEVELOPING A MASTERY PERSPECTIVE

On the basis of my experience with many athletes at many different levels of ability, I think it is important for parents and coaches to help children develop a mastery perspective toward sports. Although an ego orientation is a natural way of approaching competition, by itself it leaves the young athlete vulnerable to sharp drops in self-confidence based on comparisons with others. A mastery perspective allows the young athlete to accept failures and learn from them, to focus on improvement and not just on winning.

Sport psychology researchers such as Joan Duda have found that the motivational climate characteristic of an athletic program can greatly affect young athletes. For example, young gymnasts who train in gyms that have an ego orientation climate are more likely to develop eating disorders than athletes training in gyms with a strong mastery orientation climate. This climate is fostered by the manner in which adults organize the training experience for young athletes. The ways in which coaches and administrators set goals for the athletes, group the athletes by ability level, evaluate the athletes, and reward the athletes all affect the motivational climate of the youth sports program. Creating a healthy climate for young athletes should be an important goal of all youth sports programs.

This doesn't mean that coaches and parents should attempt to suppress an ego orientation in a young athlete. An ego orientation combined with a mastery orientation is likely to produce a committed, persistent athlete. The important thing is to help all athletes develop a mastery perspective.

This development of mastery and ego perspectives is a gradual process of increasing maturity. First, children need to be able to make the intellectual distinction between effort and ability. This happens for most children only after about age eleven. Second, children must become more realistic in their judgments of their own sporting ability. Their early confidence comes to be replaced by more realistic appraisals of their special talents. Children realize they are good at some things but not at others. Third, children gradually develop their own internal criteria for judging how well they perform on different sports tasks. They move from dependence on what adults tell them to making comparisons with other children and finally to being able to judge themselves based on effort and performance.

How can adults help children develop a mastery perspective through participation in youth sports programs?

Countering the Ego Orientation

Sport psychology provides a new way of looking at the question, How competitive is this child? There are at least two ways in which a young athlete can be competitive. First, children can develop an ego orientation to competition. This is probably what we normally mean by being competitive. The athlete wants to win, wants to be better than others, and wants to look like a winner. Such motivation can be a driving force for achievement, but it is unstable if not balanced by some degree of mastery orientation.

The athlete who looks at sports primarily as a vehicle of social comparison, which is typical of an ego orientation, is subject to strong pressures outside her control. Too often I have seen sports have a destructive rather than a constructive effect on such an athlete. She cares greatly about what others think of her, and her self-confidence becomes linked to how well she performs. When this athlete is playing well, she is on top of the world. She feels confident and seems to love to play. As long as such an athlete believes that she has high ability, her motivation and confidence are high.

But when the highly ego-oriented athlete encounters failure, she loses confidence and her desire to play is greatly reduced. If obstacles persist, she often can see only the probability of continued failure. She is likely to drop out of the sport rather than risk looking like a loser. Without some level of mastery orientation to anchor her, she has no internal frame of reference by which to judge herself. She can't see if she is really achieving anything. She can only see that she's not as good as others. Only continued, constant success can help her stay motivated. And as we know, in sports as in life, constant success is an illusory goal.

Parents and coaches place themselves in the best position to help children get the most out of their sports experiences when they understand how children develop an ego orientation or a mastery orientation to sport. Competitive experiences teach children about the ego orientation approach to sports. It is natural to develop this viewpoint, to compare ourselves to others. But it is also crucial that children learn a mastery orientation toward sports. Without this viewpoint, sports are likely to become an unhappy experience. With a mastery perspective, young athletes can learn to judge their own progress, to set their own goals, and to take satisfaction from growth, even when defeats occur. The essence of a mastery orientation is that it allows young people to think critically and independently about their own performance. This is a vital skill to have, in both sports and life.

Of course, for parents to teach their children the basics of a mastery orientation to sports, they must have some level of a mastery approach themselves. How does one develop a mastery orientation? The place to start is to evaluate the goals you set. Those with a strong ego orientation and little mastery orientation tend to be poor goal setters. Because their goals involve social comparison, they tend to focus on beating others, on winning a competition. A mastery orientation, on the other hand, involves working toward achievable results and developing a specific plan for reaching long-term objectives.

Now matter what orientation a young athlete has to competition, my philosophy is that there are a set of skills the athlete will need in order to be successful at setting and reaching her goals. These goal-setting skills can be taught, modeled, and practiced. An athlete with a strong ego approach might need to learn how to use effective short-term goals and how to use other types of feedback besides social comparison. An athlete with low ego orientation might need to learn how to use feedback from the results of competition in an effective manner. Complete the exercise in Exhibit 7.1 to see how sound your goal-setting skills are.

I don't know whether adults with a low mastery orientation can pass on a mastery perspective to children, but I suspect it is difficult. Children learn much more from observing how the adults around them behave than they do from listening to what adults tell them. If parents or coaches have a low mastery orientation, they are unlikely to display the sorts of goal-setting behaviors I have been discussing. Children are therefore unlikely to see many of the behaviors that will model a mastery orientation for them. That is why I strongly encourage the parents and coaches I work with in sports workshops to examine their own attitudes toward competition. I

Exhibit 7.1. How Strong Are Your Goal-Setting Skills?

Take the following self-test of your goal-setting skills.
Circle your answer to each question.

1. In competitive situations I have specific goals.	YES	NO
2. When I set a goal for myself, I make a plan for reaching it.	YES	NO
3. I like to win, but I also have competitive goals that have nothing to do with winning.	YES	NO
4. When I set a goal, I evaluate how well I do in reaching it.	YES	NO
5. I ask for feedback from others to see how much progress I'm making.	YES	NO
6. I strive for personal improvement.	YES	NO
7. When facing a difficult project, I set realistic but challenging goals.	YES	NO
8. I set myself very clear, specific, and measurable goals.	YES	NO
9. I set goals for myself at work and play, but I forget to follow up on them.	YES	NO
10. I don't set goals. I just go out and do it.	YES	NO

Scoring: Give yourself a point if you answered yes to questions 1 through 8, and a point for answering no to questions 9 and 10.

If you scored 1–3: You could benefit from learning more about effective goal-setting.
If you scored 4–6: You could still improve your goal-setting skills.
If you scored 7–10: Your score indicates you understand effective goal setting and are in a good position to pass that skill on by your example.

believe it is essential that adults understand their own competitive orientation and how to set effective goals if they are to help children learn to excel and improve in sports.

Teaching Young Athletes a Mastery Focus

Adults can influence the young athletes they work with by a variety of behaviors that foster and reward a mastery approach to competition.

The parent who wishes to encourage his child to develop a mastery orientation to sports can help by reinforcing effective goal setting whenever possible. Such reinforcement emphasizes to the young athlete the importance of becoming an independent judge of progress, of not always relying on comparison with others, of developing the ability to set goals and achieve them, and of the values of hard work and persistence. Here are some suggestions for ways in which parents can help foster in their child a mastery orientation toward sports.

Get Good Coaching

The type of coaching that children receive as they learn a sport is critical in shaping their attitudes toward competition. Whether it is the parent or another adult doing the coaching, the behavior of the coach will have a profound influence on the young athlete.

Some characteristics I have seen in excellent youth sports coaches over the years include the following:

Love of the game. Youngsters who are attracted to basketball or swimming love the game. They enjoy it. They desire to become better at it. The best coach to have is a role model who demonstrates his or her own love of the game. A coach who shows that she really enjoys basketball or swimming will pass her passion on to many young athletes. But a coach who is burned out or disenchanted with a sport can turn many young people away from that activity. A passionate coach helps to kindle within the young athlete the sparks of desire to master the sport.

Knowledge of the game. A coach can be committed and enthusiastic, but without the technical ability to help the child learn new skills, a coach cannot help the child improve. The knowledge of how to learn new skills and how to become proficient at them is essential to the development of the mastery approach.

This area is probably one of the biggest problems in most youth sports programs. Many coaches have very little training or knowledge in how to coach effectively, especially at the recreational level. Many volunteer parent-coaches don't even know many drills or coaching strategies. Youth sports organizations can help tackle this problem by training all coaches in the fundamentals of the sport and in effective coaching approaches. Brief programs can be offered that even busy parent-coaches will find helpful in coaching young children.

Coaches who have learned, through experience or training or both, to be effective in helping young athletes will display the following behaviors in their coaching:

- Using skill-building drills at practice. Good drills make practice sessions fun and add variety to training.

- Reinforcing correct skills. A good coach will notice when a child performs a skill correctly and will reward the child verbally or with increased attention.

- Correcting mistakes. Effective coaching involves noticing when the young athlete performs a skill incorrectly and showing or teaching the athlete how to do it right. Ignoring mistakes limits improvement.

Several programs exist to help youth sports coaches develop their effectiveness. One of the best is the Coach Effectiveness Training program, which has delivered over 250 workshops to 12,000 youth and high school coaches.

Ability to encourage. A coach can give technical feedback to a child, but whether or not the child hears the coaching often depends on how the information is presented. If feedback is given in a negative manner ("I can't believe how many times I've shown you that move. Keep your darn glove down when you move into the ball"), the child will hear the negativity but will likely tune out the correction. The same information presented in an encouraging fashion ("Good hustle. Remember next time to keep your glove down low as you move into the ball") is much more likely to be heard and acted on by the child.

Love of teaching. The mastery approach to competition deemphasizes winning and emphasizes achievement and skill building. A coach must be a good teacher to help children learn this approach. It is easy to have fun while coaching a winning team. It is more difficult to enjoy working with a struggling team and to take pleasure from the little victories that come from seeing a child learn a new skill or make a breakthrough in understanding. Good coaches are good teachers.

Of course there will be certain things that *you* look for in finding a good coach for your child. Interpersonal factors, such as good communication with parents, are also important. But I believe that the qualities just discussed form the bedrock for any effective approach to coaching young athletes.

Emphasize Progress, Not Results

The structure of competition focuses our attention on the final outcome, but this is often a very poor indicator of performance, particularly in team sports. A young athlete may play very well and still lose the game, and may also play poorly but still win over a weaker opponent. Similarly, a child may play a great game but be on a losing team, or play badly on a winning team. If only results are emphasized ("Did you win?" "How many points did you score?"), the child may not learn to judge his own performance accurately.

Coaches can set an example in this respect. In noncompetitive youth leagues, coaches can insist that all children get a chance to contribute to the team. Highly talented athletes who might otherwise dominate a game can be placed in supporting roles at times, to give other athletes a chance to play. Coaches must resist the temptation to play the biggest and best athletes all the time in order to secure a team win. Which is the greater success? A team that wins its league but in which half the players don't come back the next year? Or a team that doesn't win but in which the children make progress, have fun, and all want to play the next year?

Reward Skill Improvement

Parents and coaches can help foster a mastery orientation by rewarding children for skill development. It is easy to hand out trophies for winning and for the best players, but it is more challenging to find ways to encourage a focus on skill building. The best youth sports coaches I have observed over the years always find ways to do this. They give weekly rewards to the kids who have made the most progress that week; they reward effort and good attitude; they hug children for trying, yell encouragement when kids are tired, and constantly set a good example by being enthusiastic; they pay attention when children show that they have learned a new skill; and at all times they look for ways to reward and encourage a mastery focus in their young athletes.

Encourage Critical Self-Observation

One of the distinguishing characteristics of the athlete who has a high level of mastery is the ability to judge his own performance, independent of the results of a competition. I have observed in all the successful athletes I have worked with this ability to reflect critically on their own performance and identify areas that need improvement.

There is a big difference between being critical and being negative. Unfortunately, many athletes fall into the trap of becoming perfectionists. They strive for the unobtainable—perfection—and are very hard on themselves when they make mistakes. A successful athlete will honestly recognize when she has made a mistake, but she will then work hard to correct it. A perfectionist will beat herself up over every mistake, and this habit will gradually wear away her emotional energy and leave her frustrated, helpless, and close to burnout. This negativity is not necessary to be self-critical.

Coaches and parents can help children reflect on their own performance. Questions such as "How was that for you?" "How did you feel doing that?" "What were you thinking of while you did that skill?" "What did you notice while you were doing that?" and "Tell me what just happened" will help a child learn to reflect on her own performance. A good coach will not always give the child an answer to a problem. A good coach helps a child *discover* the solution. In this way a mastery orientation is developed. The child learns the joy of self-discovery. He realizes that progress depends on his own efforts. And he truly learns, rather than doing something just because he was told to.

A young athlete's competitive orientation to sports will influence her in so many ways throughout her sporting career. A strong ego orientation will make her competitive and she will strive to win, but she will also need a mastery orientation to help her achieve her goals. With a mastery focus, the young athlete is likely to be persistent, self-motivated, and a high achiever. Many of the worst problems in youth sports today (such as dropping out, eating disorders, and exploitation) can be greatly lessened by increasing the emphasis on mastery and deemphasizing the ego orientation aspects of sports programs.

This orientation to competition will emerge during early adolescence, but the groundwork for a child's attitude to competition is laid many years before. From his first exposure to sports and competition, a child's attitudes will be influenced by the ways his parents and coaches behave. Parents can help children develop a mastery approach to sports (and life) by understanding how children become competitive and by rewarding and encouraging the child's independent use of goals to focus on progress and improvement. No matter what a young athlete's competitive orientation, it is important that they learn effective goal-setting skills in order to make progress toward their long-term objectives.

As children grow up, they typically participate in more highly competitive programs, in school and in sports. Young people compete to get into the best schools and to play on the best teams. What effect does all this competition have on children's character and self-esteem?

HOW COMPETITION AFFECTS CHILDREN

Critics argue that many highly competitive youth sports programs exploit children for the benefit of parents. After observing elite young gymnasts and figure skaters for several years, reporter Joan Ryan questioned "our willingness to sacrifice a few medals for the sake of their health and well-being. . . . We expect sacrifices to be made in the name of great success. But when the sacrifices mean a childhood spent in the toils of physical and psychological abuse, the price is too high." The increasing intensity of competition among younger and younger children seems to play a significant role in the behavior of parents who become overly concerned with winning, at the expense of health and safety concerns.

One of the most important questions we can ask is, What effect will participation in competitive sports have on my child? It is a question I am frequently asked, in many different ways. My son seems more rough and volatile at home since the ice hockey season began. Could the sport be changing him? My daughter seems obsessed with winning at gymnastics. Do you think the competitive program she is in is good for her? My son has a new coach in tennis and suddenly he doesn't seem to like the game anymore. Sometimes he cries after practice. Should he stop? All these questions have, at heart, the question, How do competitive youth sports affect children?

There are three answers to this question. There is the negative point of view, which holds that competition is a very bad influence on children, to be avoided wherever possible. There is the positive point of view, which holds that by participating in competitive youth sports children learn wonderful life values such as teamwork, honesty, and sportsmanship. And there is the "real answer." Let's take a look at each point of view in turn.

THE NEGATIVE POINT OF VIEW: COMPETITION IS BAD FOR CHILDREN

There are those who argue that any form of competition is so negative in its effects that we should strive to get rid of competition in all its forms, including competitive sports. One of the chief proponents of this view is Alfie Kohn, who states his case in the book *No Contest: The Case Against Competition*.

Kohn makes several compelling arguments against competition, and it is worthwhile to consider them carefully. First, he argues that competition produces inferior performance. He argues that people tend to perform better when they perform alone or cooperatively with others. Competitive environments such as sports, argues Kohn, actually hurt performance. "So far from making us more productive, then, a structure that pits us against one another tends to inhibit our performance" (p. 50).

A second argument made by Kohn is that competition always produces losers, and that the experience of losing is damaging to a person's self-esteem. "Losing is always possible and often anticipated. It is an inherent part of competition, and thus there is reason to think competition is always psychologically damaging to some degree" (p. 110). Further, Kohn argues that the experience of success does not boost self-esteem. "Winning fails to satisfy us in any significant way and thus cannot begin to compensate for the pain of losing" (p. 111).

Finally, Kohn argues that competition is an inherently unpleasant experience, and as such it takes the fun out of any activity that becomes competitive. "The pure pleasure of competitive triumph is first cousin to the pleasure of punching someone in a state of manic excitement. . . . This is a pleasure we should not nurture and encourage. . . . We would do better to take our enjoyments from more constructive pursuits" (pp. 90–91). This view leads Kohn to the conclusion that we should get rid of competitive sports for children, because it stops them from having fun. Kohn deplores "the excessive competitiveness of children's athletic programs, such as Little League baseball. The spectacle of frantic, frothing parents humiliating their children in their quest for vicarious triumph is, of course, appalling. . . . These experiences with competition are so unpleasant as to lead uncounted children to leave sports permanently" (pp. 91–92).

Kohn's central thesis is accurate and undeniable. Competition is a powerful emotional experience that is likely to have an impact on self-esteem and enjoyment. His argument that these effects are always negative, however, deserves closer scrutiny.

A REPLY TO THE ARGUMENT THAT COMPETITION IS BAD FOR CHILDREN

There is some evidence to address each of the three main points raised by Kohn.

Does Competition Lead to Inferior Performance?

Does competition really hurt performance? Kohn argues that some researchers have found that performance deteriorates in competitive situations. Yet many who have studied excellence have found the opposite to be true. In fact, one of the very earliest experiments ever conducted in sport psychology concerned this question. In 1898, psychologist Norman Triplett compared the times of cyclists who performed alone with those of cyclists who were paced by other cyclists. He found that the cyclists were faster when they raced against others. This classic study was one of the first to point to the benefits of superior performance produced under competitive conditions.

As I write this chapter, I have been watching the 1998 Winter Olympic Games in Nagano. At the speed skating rink, world records are being set every night. The best athletes in the world are pushing each other to amazing levels of performance on the world stage. This is happening *because* of competition. These athletes would not be as motivated and would not have prepared as thoroughly for any other race. It is the Olympic competition that propels them. This cooperative aspect of competition—that great athletes achieve better performances when they are challenged by their competitors—is usually ignored by the critics of competition.

Psychologist Howard Gardner has taken a much broader approach to understanding expertise and excellence. In his work, he has tried to describe the actual creative process, answering the question, What does it take to be creative? One of his major findings, described in *Creating Minds*, is that true creativity can be judged only by comparing a person's work to that of others. There is no way to decide if a work, or a piece of art, or a mathematical model, is creative until it competes for attention against other similar works. Only then will the best, most significant work emerge. In other words, *excellence must emerge through competition*. He believes that only by comparisons can we tell what is good and what isn't. Gardner says, "But the crucial point here is that nothing is, or is not, creative in and of itself. Creativity is inherently a communal or cultural judgment" (p. 36).

A weak point in Kohn's analysis is that he does not look at the effect of attitudes toward competition. As indicated in Chapter Seven, the attitude an athlete takes toward competition is crucial. It makes all the difference how much you will enjoy competition, and it probably helps to determine your level of performance in the long-run. Kohn ignores all the research that demonstrates how important the competitive attitude can be.

Kohn sees competition as always involving an ego attitude. He describes competition as "beating others" rather than as trying to do something better than others do it. But researchers who have studied this issue carefully have clearly found two types of attitudes—ego and mastery. If athletes had purely an ego attitude, they would take a win any way they could get it. But most top athletes are not satisfied by having a victory simply handed to them. They want to earn it. This is the mastery orientation.

The competitive urge is crucial for high-level performance. Without it, mediocrity reigns supreme. But the attitude you adopt toward competition is very important. A high ego orientation combined with a low mastery orientation is likely to produce inferior performance. Excellent performance over the long-term seems to be a product of having a strong mastery focus. The challenge in youth sports programs is not to get rid of competition but to help children and adolescents develop effective attitudes and approaches to it.

Does the Experience of Competition Damage Self-Esteem?

A second argument made by Kohn is that competition always produces losers, and that the experience of losing is damaging to a person's self-esteem. In fact, Kohn argues that the competitive urge does not reflect a desire to be good at something but rather a way of making up for having low self-esteem. "I would offer the proposition that we compete to overcome fundamental doubts about our capabilities and, finally, to compensate for low self-esteem" (p. 99).

Kohn makes a good point that we should stop to think about the impact of winning and losing on the self-esteem and self-confidence of children. But the picture is more complex than he paints it. For one thing, children younger than eight years old make no distinction between physical ability and intellectual ability as contributors to their self-esteem. This suggests that there is a danger of a more global impact on self-esteem from losing experiences for young children. But by the time children are twelve years old, they base their self-esteem on such diverse areas as school, athletics, appearance, social acceptance, and their conduct. So for older children, a perception that they have low athletic ability, perhaps derived from losing, might be expected to affect only their physical self-esteem. Also, researchers have found that young athletes are more confident when they have a strong belief in their physical ability, regardless of winning or losing. This suggests that it is important for coaches to help young athletes develop a positive belief in their physical abilities.

Is it possible to protect children from the experience of loss? Kohn seems to have a hard time with losing in general. Perhaps with the best of intentions, he seems to want to protect all children from the experience of losing. I happen to believe that learning to deal with loss can be a valuable aspect of the youth sports experience.

Is Competition an Unpleasant and Unenjoyable Experience?

The final nail that Kohn tries to hammer into the competition coffin is his argument that competition is such an anxiety-provoking and unpleasant experience that very few people enjoy it, and even those who say they do are really attracted to the notion of boosting their egos by defeating others.

This notion surely runs counter to the experiences of millions of families who, week by week, look forward to their participation in youth sports programs. We have already seen that when you ask children directly, the number one reason they give for playing sports is *because it is fun*. Ask the young soccer player, the junior golfer, or the age-group swimmer what they think of competition, and many will tell you how much fun it is, how much they enjoy it, and how they look forward to their competitions with keen anticipation. Parents discover early that it is sometimes difficult for children to focus on the practice time necessary to build skills in a sport because children always seem to want to "play a game," that is, to compete.

Many children enjoy competitions. But not all do. Many of my young clients have been athletes who enjoyed playing a sport but were distressed by the prospect of competing. The important question is, What conditions promote enjoyment in competition, and what conditions promote anxiety?

Researchers have conducted many surveys to determine whether youth sports produce anxiety, how much they produce, and whether children enjoy their sports experiences. Tara Scanlan, for example, a sport psychology researcher at the University of California at Los Angeles, has spent many years investigating why children play youth sports, why they persist, and why they leave. She has found that young athletes report a host of reasons for their continued participation over time, and that they report a great deal of *enjoyment* from their sports involvement. Their sources of enjoyment include learning new skills and improving their existing skills, working toward mastery goals ("I enjoyed working on something so hard, to get it perfect"), gaining a sense of accomplishment from achieving their goals, having opportunities to establish friendships in the sport, traveling, striving to win, pleasing an audience, receiving social recognition for their accomplishments, and all the special thrills associated with playing the sport, inventing new moves, working hard, and concentrating deeply.

One encouraging aspect of this research is that it appears that for many children, youth sports programs deliver on their promise. Young athletes say that they play sports because they want to make friends and learn skills, and many of them do so.

Other researchers have measured the anxiety level experienced by children when competing in sports. Their findings are that the highest level of anxiety reported by a group of nine- to fourteen-year-old boys was during band solos, followed by participation in wrestling and gymnastics. Competitive team sports such as football and baseball rated lower anxiety levels than school classroom tests. This suggests that contrary to Kohn's notion, it is not just competition that produces anxiety, but evaluation. Anxiety occurs whenever children realize that their performance is being evaluated. Individual performance situations may be more stressful than team events because the evaluation is perceived to be focused solely on the individual, not on teammates as well. Even though competitive team sports are no more anxiety evoking than other common experiences such as test taking, this research does indicate that children do experience stress and anxiety during competitive sports, and the appropriate question is, Is this anxiety harmful and can children learn to cope with such stress?

Experts who have looked at this question have found that some children who experience high anxiety levels in competition do suffer negative consequences. High levels of anxiety can reduce enjoyment of sports, increase the likelihood of dropping out, hurt performance, and lead to increased risk of illness and injury. The good news is that children can learn very effective strategies for dealing with anxiety. Also, research has shown that training coaches, including training in how to reduce stress on athletes, reduces the competitive anxiety experienced by young athletes during a season. I would guess that such training might also help parents learn to alleviate the competitive anxiety of their children.

Finally, another body of evidence that indicates that competitive sports can be intensely enjoyable comes from the work of University of Chicago psychologist Mihaly Csikszentmihalyi, introduced in Chapter Four, and his colleagues. For several decades, Csikszentmihalyi has tried to discover what makes people happy. His basic finding is that trying to be happy is useless. In fact, most so-called recreational activities, such as watching television, tend to make us unhappy. Instead, he has found that happiness is the consequence of total involvement in a challenging activity of your choice. He calls this state of involvement and intense focus *flow*. As I described in Chapter Four, to achieve flow, one needs both a challenge and the skills necessary to meet that challenge. Sports are an excellent vehicle for promoting such challenges, and Csikszentmihalyi discusses many examples of athletes achieving the state of flow. In fact, by beginning sporting activities in childhood, children can increase their opportunities to experience flow, because they can develop higher skill levels and set themselves greater challenges as they gain experience.

Overall, Kohn's judgment that competition is an unnecessary evil seems overly harsh in view of the available evidence. Kohn has shown that competition *can* produce negative consequences. On this I agree, but I hope I have shown that there are also a variety of ways to transform competitive situations into skill-building rather than esteem-destroying situations.

Several factors, such as one's attitude to competition, the manner in which competition is organized, and the behavior of important adults such as parents and coaches, can all contribute to making competition either worthwhile or hurtful. The current crisis in youth sports will be resolved only if we dedicate ourselves to ensuring that youth sports programs are indeed worthwhile, and by working together to eliminate destructive attitudes and behaviors. If Kohn has helped alert us to the potential dangers of competitive programs for young athletes, he has made a worthwhile contribution to the debate.

In the next section, I examine the arguments of those who take the opposite viewpoint—that youth sports programs are inherently good for children.

THE POSITIVE POINT OF VIEW:
COMPETITION BUILDS CHARACTER

The tradition of championing sports as the foundation for building character is a long and rich one. Two centuries ago, the Duke of Wellington is supposed to have said that the Battle of Waterloo was won on the playing fields of Eton, a reference to the perceived virtues that young Englishmen received through their sporting experiences at the private school of Eton. (One might argue that the common foot soldier, who was not educated at such private schools, was the real hero of this battle, but that's another story.) Today, there are many who advocate the benefits of youth playing organized sports, particularly in corporate America, where the sports-related values of teamwork, commitment, sacrifice, and achievement are strongly advocated. An argument I have heard with increasing frequency of late is that young girls should be encouraged to play team sports because it will help prepare them for the challenges they will face in their future corporate lives.

Those who extol the benefits of youth sports programs often point to the values that are supposed to be learned through the sports experience. Some of the many values that are thought to be gained include sportsmanship, teamwork, motivation, honesty, courage, sacrifice, humility, respect, commitment, competitiveness, and drive. Descriptions of how these values are passed on to young people are often vague, and usually center on personal anecdotes like, "When I played for Coach T, I learned the value of hard work, and that's what sports can do for kids today!"

Unfortunately for the proponents of youth sports as a sure-fire vehicle for promoting character development and the acquisition of prosocial values, the evidence suggests an often contrary viewpoint. Researchers have found that the longer athletes stay involved in sports, the *less* sportsmanship they display. And researchers have found a higher incidence of problems such as eating disorders and alcohol abuse among athletes than nonathletes.

MORAL DEVELOPMENT IN SPORTS

How the youth sports experience affects moral development has been of great interest to several sport psychology researchers. As we have seen, their studies show that over time, young athletes tend to display lower levels of sportsmanship than they began with. This suggests that perhaps the more a child plays sports, the greater is the chance that he will be exposed to situations that encourage disregard for sportsmanship.

Jim, a former client of mine, gave a compelling account of an incident he was involved in when he was sixteen. He was the standout pitcher on his high school team, and in one game against their archrival one of the players on his team was struck by an opposing pitcher. Jim's coach told him to go out in the next inning and "knock down" (or try to hit) the next batter he faced. Jim didn't want to do this.

"It really tore me up," he told me. "My parents raised me not to fight violence with violence, but my coach really wanted me to go out and try to hurt the kid I was pitching to. I couldn't do it. I just couldn't bring myself to throw at his head on purpose. When I came into the dugout after the inning, the coach cursed me out in front of everyone. He said I was a coward." Jim was still upset by the incident three years later. His baseball experience was never the same after this incident. The coach refused to put Jim in as a starter anymore, and his confidence went down dramatically. He stopped playing baseball after his junior year in high school.

It is not hard to see how such experiences might shape the values of young people. If a coach, or a parent, rewards a player for placing winning as a higher priority than acting in a moral manner, the player is more likely to behave in ways that support the attempt to win at all costs. The researchers who have surveyed athletes have found exactly this result. Younger athletes have little trouble deciding that what Jim was asked to do was wrong, but by the time athletes reach high school, more of them are likely to view the coach's request as acceptable. And when athletes attain the level of collegiate and professional sports, they are likely to view unsportsmanlike acts with tolerance if they are "part of the game." Thus, with increasing experience as athletes, young people are more likely to report that they will behave with less consideration of sportsmanship.

Positive Deviance

Sport sociologists call the widespread acceptance of questionable behaviors by athletes *positive deviance*. Because sports are achievement oriented, those who participate are often likely to view the end result (winning) as a justification for the means, even if the means sometimes involves breaking the rules. Behavior that is seen as clearly deviant in other segments of society (such as drug taking) might be viewed as acceptable by many athletes and coaches if, for example, it helps attain a high level of sports performance (such as building strength). So, within the sporting community, the deviant behavior is seen in a positive light. The general public is also often willing to tolerate some of these behaviors (such as steroid abuse) in athletes because they are doing it for the good of the team (or the owner, the community, or the coach). But these behaviors, even when viewed with tolerance or perhaps support, are still dangerous. They can hurt people. Sometimes sports makes us forget this.

This trend is most pronounced among professional athletes, whose careers depend on their successful performances. It is very interesting to note that female elite athletes tended, in the past, to have significantly higher respect for sportsmanship than their male counterparts. But this difference is disappearing. Over the past few years, surveys indicate that the levels of sportsmanship reported by top female athletes are on the way down and are beginning to approach the levels displayed by elite male athletes. I wonder what this says about the value of sports as a means of preparing young women for life in the "real world"?

I think that the danger of tolerating unsportsmanlike, and sometimes outright morally wrong, behavior in professional athletes is that their actions are copied by younger athletes. Already we see that the tolerance for what used to be unacceptable behavior in college is increasing. This effect is now beginning to be seen at the high school level. And unfortunately some adults treat youth sports competition as if it were professional. Clearly, attitudes toward sports that are understandable at the professional level (win at all costs, no pain no gain) are very inappropriate at the youth sports level.

Some would argue that attitudes change as athletes become more competitive as they move up the ladder of expertise. But there are different ways to be competitive. The ego attitude might be more widespread in professional sports. But that is not a good reason to promote the ego approach in sports for children. In the long run, adults will help children far more by promoting a strong mastery approach to sports.

HEALTH PROBLEMS

Another area that should be of major concern to adults who desire to promote sports as a healthy activity is the high incidence of problems such as eating disorders and alcohol abuse in sports. Researchers have found that in some sports, such as wrestling, gymnastics, figure skating, and diving, the number of athletes with eating disorders is many times the usual rate found in the general population. The research indicates that nearly 75 percent of female collegiate athletes believe that they are overweight. The pressures of weight restrictions, the perceived bias of judges in favor of svelte athletes, and the performance demands that encourage low body fat percentages all contribute to the high incidence of disordered eating among young athletes. Athletes who are predisposed toward an eating disorder may find that the stress of youth sports precipitates the onset of the problem. It is impossible to say that sports participation promotes healthy values as long as some sports have abnormally high rates of eating disorders.

Alcohol abuse also appears to be higher in some athlete populations than in the general population. It is well known that many sports have a long tradition of promoting alcohol consumption on a social basis, but does this have an effect on actual alcohol use by athletes? Researchers have found that it may. In one study, intercollegiate athletes were found to have the highest rates of binge drinking of any group of students. In another study, by Chris Carr, male high school students in a middle-class community were found to have higher rates of alcohol use than other students. There were no differences between female athletes and nonathletes.

Such findings argue against the widely held notion that simply participating in sports promotes a healthy lifestyle. Sports participation also does not seem to promote high moral standards. This leads us to ask, Was Kohn perhaps right in suggesting that children should be protected from organized competition? Perhaps he grossly overstated the dangers of competition, but are there any valid reasons that adults should continue to support the plethora of youth sports programs we have today? Is it possible to structure competitive sports experiences so that they help children grow and develop in healthy ways?

THE REAL ANSWER: COMPETITION, CHARACTER, AND SELF-ESTEEM

I do not believe that either of the other two approaches will help us solve the crisis in youth sports. Trying to ban youth sports competitions didn't work in 1938, and it is even less likely to work today. There are too many positive effects for families to abandon youth sports. But blindly endorsing the value of competition without attempting to improve the current situation will also not move us closer to the ideal of safe, healthy, and positive sports experiences for all children.

The solution to the youth sports crisis is to recognize that our current programs are what we make them. We also have the power to change them. Sports, by itself, is value neutral. There is no guarantee that placing a child in a youth sports program will help her build character, just as there is no certainty that a competitive youth sports experience will damage a child. Whether we view competition positively or negatively depends on how the competition experience is organized, and how it affects our children and ourselves.

Adults who organize sports programs for young people must be aware of the factors that promote successful competitive experiences. We have the responsibility to structure youth sports programs that are beneficial rather than harmful. What is needed for a positive youth sports experience is thoughtful guidance by involved adults who place the developmental needs of children first and foremost.

There are four important reasons that I believe we should tackle the problems in youth sports by encouraging, not prohibiting, competitive sports for children. First, if children are taught emotional and psychological skills to help them be effective competitors, these skills will be helpful throughout life. Second, competitive sports expose children to losing. Learning how to deal with loss is a valuable experience for children. Third, competitive sports show children that there are standards of excellence in each sport. Such experience is an important part of developing a mastery orientation. Finally, competitive youth sports programs provide children with the opportunity to learn new skills and work on existing skills, to set goals and try to achieve them, and to work with others in team situations. These experiences can be fundamental in providing children with a sense of self-esteem. Good physical self-esteem can help children develop fitness and health habits, which build a strong foundation for an active and healthy life. Good sports programs can be a wonderful vehicle for giving children self-confidence. Let's look at these four points in greater detail.

Teaching Children Life Skills

Competition is everywhere in our society. From birth to the grave, we compete for the things we want and need in life. There is no doubt that competition can sometimes have negative effects on individuals, but those who haven't learned the skills to compete successfully are at the greatest disadvantage.

Think about all the ways in which competition touches our lives:

- Parents compete for scarce spots in preschool for their child

- Children compete for the top grades in school

- High school graduates compete for positions in college

- College graduates compete for the best jobs

- Companies compete for employees with special skills

- Workers compete for promotions

- Businesses compete for lucrative contracts

- Cities compete to lure companies to their region

- Countries compete for exports in a global market

Far from always being a negative process, competition can also bring out the best in us. It is often the crucible for progress. Without competition, there would be no drive to paint a more beautiful picture or build a better mousetrap. If we look around the world, we see that our country has thrived because of the benefits of competition.

Sport psychologists have identified certain *coping skills* that help young athletes deal with some of the inevitable stresses of competition. These skills are used by good athletes to increase their self-control. Steven Danish of Virginia Commonwealth University has for many years conducted programs for school-age children called Go for the Goal! These programs teach young people how to set and achieve goals in sports, academics, and life. These goal-setting skills are important for success in a competitive environment. Danish and others don't rely on hope and faith that sports will help children develop. They make it happen. There is a big difference between *teaching* children the psychological or emotional skills needed to succeed in competitive environments, and just *hoping* that a sports program will somehow promote values such as honesty and leadership.

The skills I help young athletes learn in my workshops and during consultations are concrete and specific. They can be practiced and improved. Examples of some of these coping skills include the following:

- *Knowing how to relax and calm down in pressure situations or when being evaluated.* This might involve learning how to do effective deep breathing, or practicing a method to be able to relax overly tense muscles.

- *Using one's imagination in support of reaching one's goals.* A well-developed imagination can help an athlete rehearse a difficult move, bringing about confidence and increased focus. Or it can help an athlete solve a difficult problem, as the athlete tries out several potential solutions in his mind.

- *Being able to receive and utilize criticism.* Athletes cannot improve without constructive feedback. Coaches are usually in the best position to be able to criticize an athlete's performance and provide suggestions for improvement. Athletes who become defensive might not listen to the feedback. This skill is a difficult one for many adults to learn, but it is an everyday part of sports.

- *Learning how to focus attention.* In any performance situation, there are many factors vying for attention. For example, the young athlete can focus on the score, her teammates, the coach, her parents in the stands, the crowd, the weather, or the referee. Learning to identify and focus on the key factors that help performance is a valuable coping skill. Blocking out distractions and being able to concentrate is useful in many life areas other than sports.

These are just a few examples of the many coping skills used by successful athletes. Organized competitive sport can be an excellent vehicle for teaching children how to use such skills. To help young athletes, coaches and adults involved in running youth sports programs must know how to teach children these skills. Good coaches can do this, but it may be a challenge for inexperienced coaches. This has led to a call for increased coaching education in our communities. If youth sports are worth doing, surely they are worth doing well. An important step in ensuring the success of any orga-nized youth sports experience is to have good coaches with good teaching skills.

Learning to Deal with Loss

I have already discussed Kohn's argument that competition is bad for kids because losing is always damaging to a child's esteem. He does admit at one point that it "is surely valuable to learn that one can-not always be successful" (p. 119). Kohn might be able to imagine a world with no losses and no failures, but I cannot. It is said that the more you love, the more you can be hurt by the loss of that love, but most would argue that this is not a good reason to avoid love. Simi-larly, is the possibility of failure a good reason to avoid competition? I know that I have much more admiration for the person who com-petes but fails to get a new patent, invent a new medicine, or set a world record than someone who avoids trying at all.

Competitive games for children will always generate a wide range of emotional responses, spanning the continuum of the cliché "from the thrill of victory to the agony of defeat." Sport psychologists have suggested that youth sports competition can therefore be a won-derful way to encourage children to reflect on their behaviors in emotionally intense situations. Psychologists talk about "teachable moments," which are situations in games where something signifi-cant has just happened. It might be a nasty foul, an accidental col-lision, a false start, an attempt to cheat, an unexpected loss, or one of hundreds of emotional situations that routinely occur in orga-nized sports activities for children. What usually happens is that the coaches and officials let the game continue and the moment is soon forgotten. But what would happen if all the children participating were asked to think about how *they* would have behaved in that situation? From my experience, children enjoy discussing these teachable moments, even from a young age. If adults accept their responsibility to children, and don't ignore it, they can use orga-nized sports to teach children valuable lessons about life. But this will never happen if coaches and parents focus only on the competitive structure of the game.

For more than twenty years sport psychologist Terry Orlick has been championing the cause of using sports for children as a wonderful way to teach cooperation and important values. His words eloquently sum up the value of this approach:

> Within competitive structures are countless opportunities for teaching important human values. What better place than in the midst of a game to discuss the true meaning of such values as winning, losing, success, failure, anxiety, rejection, fair play, acceptance, friendship, cooperation, and healthy competition? What better place to help children become aware of their own feelings and more sensitive to the feelings of others? What better place to encourage children to help one another learn how to cope constructively with some of the problems they face? A time-out can be called to take advantage of a meaningful learning opportunity. The value (or devaluation) can be discussed quickly, the behavior can be reinforced or a change in behavior recommended, and play can resume. With little direction, children can decide for themselves what they want to get out of a game.

The ability to identify one's emotions and to act effectively when emotional has been called *emotional intelligence* by some. There is no need to review all the research that has been done in this area, but let me suggest that organized youth sports programs offer a great opportunity to help children develop such emotional intelligence.

I was involved in a program directed by Maurice Elias of Rutgers University in the early 1980s in which we went into fourth grade classrooms and helped teach children how to stop and think before acting in emotional situations. This program was very effective. To my knowledge, similar programs have not been attempted using the basketball court and the football field instead of classrooms as learning situations, but think of how effective such interventions might be. And to those who question the practicality of such an approach, let me suggest that the best youth sports coaches have already been doing this for many, many years.

Over the years I have heard many wonderful examples of coaches teaching young athletes valuable life skills in practices and competitions. Why not help all youth sports programs to run in this manner? The ultimate responsibility to ensure that this happens lies with us, the concerned adults who make up our local communities, school districts, and volunteer organizations.

Promoting a Mastery Orientation

In the previous chapter, I described how the most effective competitors are those with a strong mastery orientation, and how those with a high ego but low mastery orientation are at risk for problems such as burnout, cheating, and inconsistent performance. It is therefore important to help children develop a mastery orientation in sports from an early age.

Whether a mastery approach to sports generalizes to other life situations, such as academics or work, is an open question. There is no definitive research addressing this issue, but on the basis of observation it appears likely. And perhaps the transfer of learning can be facilitated by coaches and parents who reinforce the mastery approach of children and show them how to use this approach in other life areas, such as academics.

To see how a mastery orientation can be fostered in a young athlete, let me describe a young golfer I worked with named Amy, whom I first met when she was fourteen years old. At age eleven, Amy became interested in golf when she saw Laura Davies on television. She admired the power and grace of Davies's game and wanted to be able to play that way. Amy began to take some coaching lessons from an experienced local pro at her town's municipal golf course. The pro taught her the fundamentals, and Amy practiced hard on her own, spending many afternoons on the driving range working on her game. At this stage, Amy simply wanted to learn how to play golf. It fascinated her, and she could see continual improvement in her game.

Notice that up until this point, competition is not present or necessary. An interest in the skill area (whether it be golf, music, or computer programming) is required to set the wheels in motion, and this interest can sustain a great deal of skill development if the person discovers that she likes the activity. But at some point, a question emerges. As her skill level increased, Amy began to ask the question, "How good am I?" She wanted to test her skill level and see how well she could play. In one sense, competition has already begun, because now Amy is comparing her performance over time. There must be some standard of excellence against which any skilled performer can measure herself. In golf, this means keeping score. Amy wanted to know how her scores compared to those of other players. "OK, I can go around this course in eighty-five strokes," Amy said to herself, "but how many strokes do other thirteen-year-old girls take? And what's the best score you can get on this course?" This is typical of the way an ego orientation develops. Notice that in Amy's case the mastery orientation came first and was followed by the growth of an ego focus.

Competition does provide performers in any given area with a way to measure their progress. Those who would argue that competition should be abolished must propose an alternative means of measuring improvement. I think that simply looking at our own performance over time is not adequate. It is too easy to be satisfied with our own performance, even if it is not very good. Expertise develops when the urge to improve, to become as good as other skilled performers, or even better than them, occurs. This urge is the ego side of the competitive instinct. But without competition, it is nearly impossible to imagine how excellence could develop.

Back to Amy, the young golfer. When she realizes that there are other golfers better than her, she becomes motivated to improve her game. Amy has become ego focused. This is a critical stage in the development of her competitive orientation. From this point her development can proceed in several different directions.

For example, her ego focus may predominate. It is easy for a young athlete's progress to be slowed by a high ego orientation. In golf, as in most sports, the game itself focuses the player's attention on the result. There is a score on every hole. The golfer always knows if she shot as well as (par), worse (bogey+), or better than expected (birdie or better). Every shot seems important. Golfers can immediately see how their playing companions are doing, and in some tournaments a leader board supplies information on the rest of the field. This focus on comparing oneself to others and keeping score paralyzes some athletes. Many others become anxious and tense under these conditions and can't play well.

This happened to Amy. When she came to see me for a consultation she was fourteen, playing in several tournaments a season, and hoping to make her school's varsity team the next year. But her confidence was gone. She felt she had made no improvement during the previous year. Her handicap had increased slightly and she was struggling in every tournament she entered. Amy had begun to approach golf competitions with dread. No longer was she thinking about how much she loved the game. Her main fear was of looking bad in front of others.

My goal was to help Amy strengthen her mastery orientation. We took several steps to achieve this. First, I had Amy fill out the Youth Sports Motivation Survey from Chapter Four. I wanted her to remember why she liked golf in the first place. When an ego focus begins to predominate, it is easy for an athlete to lose sight of her original goals. Amy identified improving her golf skills, having fun, and doing something well as her major motivations. Next we worked on setting goals to help her focus on each of these major objectives. Improving her golf skills involved spending time with her coach, working on her game at the range, and committing to her best shots on the course. With a high ego focus, Amy had begun to worry about every shot in a round, trying to prevent mistakes from happening. Now she worked on choosing the best shot for each situation, and focusing her attention on making a sweet swing.

To help herself focus on having fun, Amy learned how to relax before a round. I taught her some simple deep breathing and muscle stretching methods to help her lower her tension level. She sought out some friends to joke around with before she began a round, and on the course she reminded herself that every shot she faced was a challenge to enjoy, not a punishment for poor play.

Her final objective was a tough one for her. For some time, Amy had been having a hard time remembering how to enjoy the game. It had become hard work, and competitions were not something to which she looked forward. But as she refocused her attention on her own game, not on the play of others, she gradually rediscovered her passion for the game. A breakthrough came after she saw a movie called *Dead Poet's Society*. She identified strongly with a character in the movie and told me that in her next round she was really "alive" to what she was doing. "I looked around and enjoyed the scenery, I could smell the flowers and the trees, I felt overjoyed to be on a golf course," she laughed. She had rediscovered her enjoyment of the game, and on her own.

I believe that the steps Amy took helped her regain a mastery focus toward golf. This helped counterbalance the natural tendency to become ego oriented, which occurs as an athlete moves into more competitive levels of a sport. It is not necessary to see a sport psychologist in order to build a mastery focus. Through similar steps, parents and coaches can help a young athlete stay goal focused and achieve excellent performance.

Sports and Self-Esteem

As young children grow and develop, they face a big challenge. They must answer the question, "Who am I?" For adults, the answer to this question usually begins with reference to a career or occupation. An adult might answer by saying, "I'm Sharon, the lawyer," or "I'm Tony, the banker." Children don't have such an easy answer to the question. They must forge their own identities, starting almost from scratch. How do they do it? By finding out what makes them different from the other children around them. They must discover what they're good at.

Self-Confidence

Because physical development is such an important part of a child's experience, the mastery of physical skills is essential for the development of a well-rounded sense of identity. When a child masters a new physical skill, there is a surge of pride and confidence. "Look at me!" yells the young child learning to ride a bike, swing from a play-gym, or hit a ball thrown to her. The child is full of delight and joy. She is learning that here's something she can do by herself. Here's a new skill that belongs just to her. "I'm Sue, and I can ride a bike," she says to herself. In this way she builds her sense of who she is.

It's so important to help children be successful at this stage of learning. If they have success and fun, they quickly learn an approach to life that will stay with them forever. Children learn that they can master new skills successfully and that they enjoy trying something new. This is the foundation of self-esteem. A confident child believes that she will succeed when she comes up against a new challenge.

On the other hand, children who don't get the chance to learn new skills, or who are criticized for making mistakes, also learn an approach to life. But their approach is full of doubt and insecurity. They expect to fail when they encounter a new challenge. Learning something new is an experience they dread. These children have what psychologists call low self-esteem. What that really means is that they have learned to expect failure when they try to do something.

Perhaps you can see why I believe that sports and physical activity are very important in every child's life. Many of the challenges a child faces are physical ones: learning to walk, to ride a bike, to run, to catch, to throw. If a child learns that he is good at these things, he'll develop a confident attitude to physical activity. He'll have what psychologists call high self-esteem. But if he learns that he's no good at sports, he will have little confidence in himself. Physical activity will become something to fear. Psychologists call this having low self-esteem.

Other activities, such as learning to read, also build the young child's self-esteem, but physical activities remain the most pervasive vehicle for self-expression for many years. A child must feel in control of his own body in order to have a general sense of confidence.

Good Health

There is another very important reason why it's vital to help children enjoy physical activity from an early age. It is highly likely that many of our attitudes about fitness are shaped in these early years. Children who are repeatedly told that they have no athletic skills may tend to give up on fitness and exercise as adults. Lack of physical activity is a major cause of adult health problems. On the other hand, children who are exposed to a variety of fun-filled physical activities probably tend to remain physically active throughout life. This helps them stay fit and healthy.

The confidence that children develop through a positive introduction to sports can help them in many areas. Sport psychology researchers have found that children who learn sound sports skills and develop athletic confidence at a young age also tend to be more confident in other areas, such as the classroom. An incident from my own early experiences in youth sports illustrates this point.

As a young child I suffered from chronic bronchitis. It seemed that all sorts of common things could trigger painful attacks—pollen, fresh paint, household dust, and especially cigarette smoke blown my way by unthinking adults. The worst attacks incapacitated me. I would be confined to bed for several days, struggling to breath, while my anxious parents administered a variety of homespun remedies. Naturally my parents became cautious about my health. Like other kids my age, I wanted to play rugby, but we quickly discovered that a rugby game on a dry, dusty field was a good way to trigger another bout of coughing and wheezing. It didn't help that I was also slow to develop physical coordination. I was the kind of kid who was always dropping plates and bumping into lamps. Soon I saw myself as a sporting incompetent. When teams were chosen in the playground I was one of the last to be picked, and I soon began to avoid games and sports as much as possible.

All this changed dramatically when I was twelve years old. In one of those mysterious moments of chance that are so much a part of life, I was selected to join my high school's elite gymnastics exhibition team. Looking back, I still can't tell if the decision was a complete mistake or a piece of inspiration on the part of the teacher who coached the team. When we were freshmen in junior high, he came to our physical education class to recruit new team members. That morning I executed a perfect back handstand, the only one of my life, and he happened to see it. Just like that, I was on the team. My parents, convinced a mistake had been made, requested a meeting with Brother Pearce, the coach, but he calmed their fears and suggested a trial period to see if I could adapt to the demands of the team. So I joined.

Truthfully, I was always the least skilled member of the team. But that trial period never ended. Brother Pearce quickly realized he'd picked an athletic klutz for his team, but when he saw my joy at being one of the team members, he kept me on. He was always patient, encouraging, and persistent. I didn't master some of the elaborate routines of the real athletic stars, but I became competent at all the basic moves. Our practices were after school, and they were hard, but the camaraderie on the team made up for the difficulty of the sport. I helped with setting up all the equipment for our performances and I was proud never to miss an exhibition. Under Brother Pearce's tutelage, my body became stronger and more supple. I came to believe that I had some sporting potential after all, and I took up other sports that interested me. One of these, tennis, became a lifelong passion and a game at which I excelled.

My experiences in gymnastics, traveling around our district and putting on exhibitions at shopping malls and at school fairs, gave me new confidence in my ability to interact with others. Whereas previously I had been shy, now I became outgoing. My initial reaction to challenges changed from "I can't," to "I'll give it a try." I believe that my adult career as a sport psychologist would have been impossible if not for those happy hours spent mastering the tumbles and flips on Brother Pearce's gymnastics team. Learning from him transformed my attitude toward physical activity and gave me a totally new outlook on my own body. I can never thank him enough for his encouragement.

My own story of involvement with a caring and skilled instructor is one I've heard hundreds of times from others who have benefited from organized youth sports programs. It's a classic example of the way a good sports experience can build self-esteem. The challenge for us as concerned adults is to structure all youth sports programs so that they give young people confidence rather than tear their confidence down. The crisis we face is one of commitment. Do we have the courage to work together to solve the problems we face? Together, coaches, parents, and administrators can build wonderful programs that meet the needs of children and families, promote sportsmanship, and build pride and confidence through skill building and achievement.

Let's stop talking and do it.

POSITIVE APPROACHES
TO YOUTH SPORTS

I don't try to hide the fact that I am a strong believer in the potential value of organized sports programs for children and adolescents. I have experienced the many benefits that good programs can bring to young people. But now that I have examined the crisis facing us in youth sports, I have learned that it's not possible to shrug off the problems—emotional abuse of children; confrontational relationships among children, parents, and coaches; exploitation of athletes; injuries and eating disorders—or to blame them on "crazy parents," "cruel coaches," or "uncaring administrators." The problems run deeper than that. We are facing a crisis because of the attitudes we take toward competition, because of the way we structure our youth sports programs. Our problems are deeply imbedded in the values and attitudes that are reflected throughout our communities.

Consequently, I must ask whether there are possible solutions to the crisis. Is change possible, or are our youth sports programs doomed to repeat the patterns I have described in this book? Throughout these pages I have suggested actions that can be taken by individual parents and adults to reverse the pattern of emotional pressure common in competitive youth sports situations. But in this chapter I explore the possibilities for changing the entire nature of the programs we conduct for children and adolescents.

One potential solution has been tried, and the results were dismal. In light of the huge growth of organized sports programs for children in the last forty years, it would seem that the noted educators, physicians, and experts who attended the Atlanta Conference in 1938, mentioned in Chapter Two, failed. They wished to discourage competitive sports within the school systems for children younger than age fourteen. But as we have seen, the void they created was quickly filled by a plethora of privately administered sports programs for children. Perhaps the mistake the experts made was in discouraging competitive youth sports without encouraging a better system to be put in its place.

I think that parents are right in this respect: competitive programs for children can do a lot of good, for children, for families, and for communities. They meet very real needs, which I discussed in Chapters Three and Four. So instead of proposing to prohibit competitive sport experiences for young people, how can we organize programs that truly reflect our cherished values (not just pay them lip service) and help children grow toward independence as resourceful, moral, healthy, and self-reliant individuals while strengthening the bonds within families and communities?

HOW PARENTS CAN HAVE AN IMPACT WITHIN YOUTH SPORTS

Writing this book has been a worthwhile experience for me as a parent and educator, because it has helped me to see more clearly where the problems in youth sports lie, and in researching the book I have discovered many worthwhile programs that really put the needs of children first. I now believe that solutions to the crisis in youth sports are indeed possible. Making changes involves taking action. Here are some ideas about ways we can really take action to strengthen our organized sports programs for children.

Get Involved

First, parents must evaluate the youth sports programs in which their own children participate. There is no sense in placing a child in a youth sports program that does not address the goals of both parent and child. Second, parents and other concerned adults can take an active approach to helping organize and develop community youth sports programs that meet their needs and those of their children. If the available programs seem to foster an overly ego-oriented approach to competition, parents should seek other programs that help children to develop a mastery perspective on sports and life. If good alternatives are not available, parents might consider starting their own program.

Of course this approach is difficult. Starting a new program and doing it right is difficult. Even trying to influence existing programs to change and improve is never an easy task. Parents who attempt to change existing programs will find that they need a broad range of political and social skills. Change is rarely achieved easily, and usually requires extensive collaboration. My advice to parents is to begin with small changes and build from there. The first steps are the hardest.

Establish the Philosophy and Goals of the Community's Youth Sports Programs

There is nothing more useful for a youth sports program than a good philosophy. Without clear goals, youth sports programs are liable to drift in any direction. And if the adults concerned are not all working together to achieve the same goals, conflict is inevitable. By themselves, coaches, parents, and administrators cannot steer a decisive course for the programs they organize. From experience I know that all parties must work together.

Recently I was addressing a large gathering of parents and coaches at a nearby middle school. When I opened up a discussion following my presentation, a debate soon emerged between two groups in the school. One group of parents and coaches argued that their middle school sports programs should stick to the philosophy of "everyone participates." They felt strongly that all children enrolled in sports programs should get an equal chance to learn and play. But another group of parents argued that because the school fielded several teams in competitive leagues, it was incumbent upon the school to help the teams win. "My son works hard at basketball," stated one mother. "Why should he always have to suffer because the coach has to put some losers into the game at the end?"

This sort of debate, and these differences of opinion, are widespread in our society. People have very different views about the nature of competition, as I described in Chapter Seven. The debate in which this community, this school, was engaged was important. I believe that such debates are an essential part of establishing an effective program of sports and physical activity for children. Out of such debates a philosophy must emerge that, if not universally agreed upon, must at least reflect the values and goals of the majority. It is this philosophy that will guide the actions of coaches and parents, and in turn this philosophy will affect the children involved in many ways.

Two important questions must be addressed in determining the philosophy of a sports program for children: What is the purpose of this youth sports program? and What are the goals for the children?

There are many different answers to these basic questions. Good answers should consider the following factors:

• *The developmental needs of children.* Children's physical, emotional, and mental abilities and needs change as they develop. Good programs take these changes into account. Highly competitive programs for eight-year-olds, for example, can do more harm than good.

• *Talent development versus mass participation.* Very few children have the talent to play competitive sports at the highest level. It therefore makes sense that most programs should have as their primary goals the development of physical competence and the promotion of physical activity, fun, sportsmanship, and good health. Too often this is not the case. The needs of the many are sacrificed for the talented few.

• *Attitude toward competition.* It is easy to promote an ego-oriented approach to competition. It takes more work and planning to help children learn a mastery orientation as well. For example, the American Youth Soccer Organization (AYSO), founded in

1962, is built on five basic principles that attempt to create the best competitive environment for children. These principles are

> *Everyone plays.* AYSO mandates that every player on every team *must* play at least half of every game.
>
> *Open registration.* AYSO guarantees each child's participation so that he or she can experience the same benefits that any child gets from sports.
>
> *Positive coaching.* AYSO believes that negative criticism is inappropriate for coaching children, and experience shows that it doesn't produce good results. Positive coaching builds positive team spirit.
>
> *Balanced teams.* Stacked teams can have an unfair advantage. Kids have more fun when the teams are of similar ability. AYSO establishes balanced teams at the start of the season, so everyone can experience the learning that comes from winning—and losing—real games.
>
> *Good sportsmanship.* AYSO creates an environment based on mutual respect and avoids an attitude of winning at all costs. Programs are designed to generate good sportsmanship among players, coaches, and fans alike.

Every youth sports program, including school-based programs, should have published goals that you can examine before committing your child to the program.

Examine Attitudes

When an athlete who is struggling with an eating disorder or perhaps burnout comes to see me, one of the first steps I take is to help the athlete examine his or her attitudes toward sports and competition. I do the same for families who seek my advice about a conflict over a child's sports participation. If the crisis in youth sports is to be resolved, parents, coaches, and administrators must regularly examine their attitudes toward youth sports and be honest about their motives for participation.

I enjoy my work as a sport psychologist with elite athletes. When a twenty-one-year-old athlete tells me of her burning desire to make the Olympics and to be the best in her sport, I support her ambitions and try to help her achieve her goals. I know she will have to make many sacrifices on her way to the top, but I respect her right to choose that difficult road.

When a ten-year-old athlete tells me he wants to be on the Olympic team, my reaction is very different. First, I realize that the child has little ability to be realistic about his chances of reaching that level of performance. Many children at this age believe they can be the next Michael Jordan or Shaquille O'Neal. Second, I am very suspicious of the sacrifices a child of this age might be making in support of his dream. I have seen far too many cases of burnout, overtraining, and injury among young athletes to believe that a very competitive approach to sports is the best way to support a young athlete's dreams.

It is one thing for an adult to make a decision to train four hours a day, to pay for the best coaching, and to go on a special diet to reach the top in his sport. It is quite another thing for a parent to make those decisions on behalf of a child. Too often, as I have described, the parent is blinded by personal ambition and is unrealistic about the child's talent level or motivation, or both. There are some incredibly talented athletes who deserve the support needed to reach their potential. But even in these cases there is no need to place the young athlete in the types of exploitive programs that we have allowed to flourish in support of a supposed pursuit of excellence.

I wish that all parents could speak with the many young athletes I have seen over the years—with the successful ones, who have often achieved great success by a careful and balanced approach to youth sports participation, avoiding the problems I have discussed in these pages with the help of wise parents; and with the many athletes who have suffered because of an overcommitment to a narrow definition of success, who have paid the price for their pursuit of fleeting victories and triumphs.

The glittering prizes that so many parents today want their children to achieve often turn out to be empty shells. Is it worth pushing children hard to achieve such goals? Parents must become better informed about what happens to young athletes in the present sports system. And they must help children develop the inner strength and self-confidence to stand up and say, "No, I will not be used and abused" when they find themselves in a bad situation.

Educate Participants

Some of the problems in youth sports today are directly caused by the attitudes of parents, coaches, and administrators. To change attitudes, something needs to happen to encourage people to think about the issues that have been raised in this book. An ongoing education effort within a youth sports program will encourage all participants to consider these issues seriously. Program developers can share the program philosophy with parents in written form, ask parents to sign up to support the goals of the program, and hold support meetings to promote sportsmanship (invite speakers to attend: coaches, former players, experts, and so on).

Involve the Children in Decisions

I have argued strongly that the needs and goals of children must be attended to in order to build a successful youth sports program. What better way to do this than to include children in the development and coordination of programs?

To those who would argue that children are too young to be involved in such matters, I say that this is an excellent way to teach children responsibility. When a range of ages can be included in the program, older children can serve as role models for younger children in learning how to work with adults to develop the best youth sports programs.

Some programs have already successfully taken the step of including children in their decision-making process. For example, the A Sporting Chance Foundation in Chicago has a Girl's Advisory Board that has a voice in the design and development of programs. The foundation provides programs to girls ages seven to seventeen, and seeks to develop leadership and lifelong health in girls through participation in sports. Keisha, age sixteen, says of the program, "I love how everyone encourages you and supports you. No one puts you down or makes you feel like a failure. I also love how everyone is like family and you don't have to feel intimidated by anyone."

Teach Both Sports Skills and Life Skills

Using sports as a vehicle for teaching children valuable life lessons has long been a goal, stated or implied, of most organized youth programs. But the evidence suggests that far from encouraging sportsmanship, prolonged exposure to sports actually results in less commitment to values such as fair play. To reverse this trend, youth sports programs must actively teach children the skills they seek to promote. For example, if leadership and teamwork are two major goals of a program, each child must receive learning experiences in how to be a leader and how to cooperate in a team setting. Children will not learn such skills simply by exposure to team sports. Some suggestions for increasing the value of sports as a learning experience for children are

- Use teachable moments to illustrate important sports lessons

- Use team discussions to help resolve conflicts

- Reinforce examples of sportsmanship and fair play

- Teach skills such as goal setting and staying calm under pressure within the sports setting—not as an academic exercise removed from the child's actual sports experience

Allocate Resources to Support Community and Social Goals

Consider this puzzle. Go to any playground for young children in your area. What do you observe? Children on the go! They run across the sand, they leap from the bars, they swing to the skies, and they shout and yell and laugh the entire time. It's not just a few children who play—over time they all get involved. The energy and enthusiasm that young children have for action leaves most parents breathless.

Now freeze this scene in your mind and fast forward some thirty years into the lives of these children. The young kids are now young adults. Do they still go to the playground? Of course not! Do they still have that enormous energy? It's hard to tell. Nearly all of them have full-time jobs, and they work very hard at their careers. Most of these young people have started their own families, and they seem to work hard there, too. But not many of them still get out and run around as energetically as they did when they were children. Only about a third of them get regular exercise, and even fewer are still involved in sports. A few run, some jog, some ride bikes, and others engage in such sports as tennis, skiing, and golf. The rest? Well, they seem to use up most of their energy commuting back and forth to work, running errands in their cars, and exercising their fingers on the TV channel changer.

What happened? Where did all that enormous energy and zest for life go? What on earth could have taken place in those thirty years that changed such an energetic group of kids into such a sedentary bunch of adults?

Certainly there are some legitimate reasons why adults in America don't play and exercise in great numbers. The time demands of modern life are great, it is difficult to create opportunities to get out and be active. But I believe that a major reason that so many adults lead inactive lifestyles is because of the elitist way we treat sports and play in America. We encourage our children to get involved in sports in huge numbers, then we keep restricting their opportunities to participate. By late adolescence, only a few are still playing. Instead, we train our children to worship the "great" athletes on television, we teach them to be spectators rather than participants, and we severely limit their chances to play the games they love. Of course, as adults they end up as passive sports followers rather than as energetic, involved athletic individuals.

Is this what you want for your child?

I've greatly enjoyed my years working with elite athletes, especially my years with the many Olympic sports in our country. But I disagree with the major philosophy of the Olympic and professional sports in this country, which is that to identify the very few elite athletes who can win medals or sustain a professional career we must first weed out all those athletes who can't reach the highest levels of performance. In the introduction to this book I called this the talent development model of sports.

In most popular mainstream sports in the United States, the talent-development model is in effect. The major sports (such as gymnastics, swimming, baseball, and so on) publicly call this a problem, and much time is spent discussing the issue of youth sports dropouts. In some sports it is estimated that about 50 percent of participants drop out each year during the teenage years. In fact, however, the talent-development model works to the advantage of major sports. Because only the most talented and committed athletes survive to the highest stages of athletic development, the system works as a talent identification program. Olympic-level or professional coaches end up training only the best athletes, who have survived the weeding out process at the lower levels of specialization.

In contrast to the existing talent-development model of sports, I would like to see us strive to create what I called the participation-promotion model of sports. This model is guided by the idea that we should strive to keep people involved in sports and physical activity throughout their lives. In this model, all the athletes involved in sports in large numbers as children would remain athletically involved into and throughout their adult years. This could be accomplished by creating more opportunities for sports participation as children grow older rather than restricting the opportunities, as is presently the case. Youth sports programs would encourage as much physical activity as possible, focusing on enjoyment and the formation of lifelong good habits instead of on winning competitions.

If we think about the big picture, the answers to the dilemma I have posed are simple. It all comes down to the behaviors we encourage and reinforce. For example, James Hill, director of the Clinical Nutrition Research Unit at the University of Colorado, argues that we actually encourage obesity in our country by providing too many opportunities to eat large quantities of food, such as fast food outlets and restaurants, and too few opportunities to exercise. He suggests that we should make physical education mandatory in schools so that children will have at least thirty minutes of vigorous exercise every day. That's a good start. But even better would be to establish youth sports programs that create lifelong intrinsic motivation in children to enjoy physical activities. Making people exercise won't work nearly as well as encouraging the natural desire of children to be playful and active.

A final anecdote might reinforce my argument. Recently I was given a guided tour of the fitness facilities of one of the largest universities in the country. Our group was proudly shown a particularly impressive weight room and gymnasium with luxurious decor and state-of-the-art equipment. I noticed that it was empty and inquired when the students used it? "Good heavens," was the reply. "This isn't for the students. This is for the football team!" What better example of how our country has gone mad in pursuit of an illusory goal of transient glory, missing the chance to achieve a worthwhile goal of fitness for all.

Respect and Support Coaches

Several critics of youth sports programs have argued that the prob-lems caused by some coaches suggest that coaches should be trained and certified before coaching children. Although this might work in some elite programs, the problem with this solution is that the vast majority of coaches for kids are volunteers. As parents, hus-bands, wives, and workers, they simply have no time for extensive training in coaching.

Although certification is probably unworkable, it is certainly possible to give more support to youth sports coaches. Such support should include assistance in developing team goals that are in keep-ing with the program philosophy; meetings with parents, at least at the beginning and end of seasons, in order to articulate program objectives and answer questions; some basic instruction in safety and in effective coaching methods; and the support of parents dur-ing the season. Coaching is a difficult job, especially as a voluntary activity, but it becomes extraordinarily difficult when there is con-flict between parents and coaches. Yet this conflict has become so widely recognized that sport psychologists have given it a name: the athletic triangle (parents, coaches, athletes). Instead of working against each other, coaches and parents serve the needs of children far better when they cooperate.

If the parents I talk to have a primary complaint against coaches, it is usually that they are unfair in some way. Often this issue re-volves around how much playing time the children are getting. Most parents naturally want to see their child get a lot of playing time. If the coaches I speak with have a primary complaint about parents, it is that they interfere too much. Coaches naturally want to be the ones that make decisions about who starts, who plays in what position, and so on, and they resent frequent input or criti-cism from parents.

Such conflict is too often the result of the way youth sports pro-gram are organized. When coaches are not given support and respect, and when they are not encouraged to set program goals collaboratively with parents, problems are almost certain to arise. I have found that such problems can be avoided if partnerships are established at the outset among coaches, parents, administrators, and athletes. For example, a community soccer program can establish a sports council consisting of several representatives for each party participating in the program, that is, some coaches, some parents, and so on. This council, or its equivalent, should have the responsibility for making sure that the goals of the program are met, and it should establish a clear program philosophy, written program goals, and a code of sportsmanship, if this hasn't already been done.

Another way to support coaches is to define a clear method of conflict resolution for dealing with problems that do arise. A written procedure will help clarify the respective roles of parents, coaches, and administrators in the event of a dispute. For example, parents should be encouraged to make an appointment first to take their concerns to the coach. Criticizing a coach immediately following a game should not be permitted. Only if the parent does not receive a satisfactory response from the coach should he or she ask to speak with a program administrator.

In return for such support, coaches should be expected to earn the respect of their players and of the community. If given the chance, most will do so. Sometimes a youth sports program will find that it has a coach who, even with support, is unable to fulfill the expectations of the program, and in that case the coach should be removed.

Develop a Sportsmanship Code of Conduct

Most programs have a code of conduct or a similar expression of the behaviors expected from athletes, coaches, officials, and fans. I have found that athletes really support this code if they are involved in developing it. For the integrity of the program, the code should be followed by everyone—no exceptions. Code violations should have clear punishments attached to them. Usually a loss of privileges (such as not playing, for an athlete, or not attending games, for a parent) is the best deterrent for the future.

Educate the Fans

Usually the parents are the fans, but I have found that it is important to address the expectations of a youth sports program for how fans behave at the competitions they conduct. Often, parents at competitions for children will behave as though they were paying fans at a professional sporting event. As I discussed in Chapter Five, this is not appropriate for the children who are participating. Program administrators and officials can work together to make sure that parents support the code of conduct as they have agreed to.

A major element of this code must be to treat one's opponents well. This humanizes competition and stops an "us versus them" mentality from developing. I suggest organizing meetings after games to promote camaraderie, organizing dinners and lunches for athletes, and hosting social events for both or all teams involved.

Model Good Behavior

Finally, I think it is important to point out that children learn a lot from observing the behaviors of their parents. If parents are strongly encouraging a child to participate in a sport but have no physical activities of their own, the child is receiving a mixed message. How can we expect children to grow up to be active and healthy adults if their parents model for them an inactive lifestyle?

I suspect that there are many psychological advantages for parents who remain actively involved in sports and physical activities. It's difficult for parents to be critical of their child's progress in a sport if the parents themselves are constantly being confronted by how difficult it is to move forward in their own sport. I know that since I have taken up golf I have gained tremendous appreciation for how difficult it is for any child to learn the complex motor and cognitive skills of a sport. This gives me more patience for helping my children.

I think that the best sports programs of the future will include the whole family. What better way for children to learn to have fun and enjoy sports than by sharing activities with their parents, siblings, and friends?

The vast majority of the organized games our children play on the field and in the gym tend to be similar to the games we see on television played by adults. There is no reason that this should be so. In fact, it often makes little sense for children to attempt to play the same games as adults. It has been difficult for us, the adults, to change this pattern. We've been trying since at least 1938. Yet parents still enjoy seeing their children compete in sports that mimic those played by professionals. In many ways, the current state of organized sports programs for children meets the needs of parents rather than those of children. It's not too late to change this state of affairs. My hope is that parent by parent, family by family, school by school, and community by community, we can change our programs to meet the needs of our children.

It will be worth the effort.

NOTES

Introduction

The findings on the activity levels of adults and the benefits of regular physical activity are contained in the report of the Surgeon General, "Physical Activity and Health" (Atlanta, Ga.: Centers for Disease Control, 1996).

Chapter One

Page 13. The research on how much practice it takes to become an expert performer is summarized in Ericsson, K.A., and Charness, N., "Expert Performance: Its Structure and Acquisition," *American Psychologist*, 1994, *49*, 725–747.

Page 13. The quote from Alan Rothenberg, president of U.S. Soccer, appeared in Foster-Simeon, E., and Brewington, P., "U.S. Soccer Gets Serious," *USA Today*, May 29, 1998, p. 13C.

Page 14. Ryan, J., *Little Girls in Pretty Boxes: The Making and Breaking of Elite Gymnasts and Figure Skaters* (New York: Warner Books, 1995), pp. 242–243.

Page 14. Peter Donnelly discussed using child-labor laws to protect young athletes in "Problems Associated with Youth Involvement in High-Performance Sports," in B. R. Cahill and A. J. Pearls (eds.), *Intensive Participation in Children's Sports* (Champaign, Ill.: Human Kinetics, 1993), pp. 95–126.

Page 19. The comprehensive survey of 1,183 athletes aged eleven to eighteen and of parents of 418 athletes aged six to ten was conducted by Sapp, M., and

Haubenstricker, J., "Motivation for Joining and Reasons for Not Continuing in Youth Sport Programs in Michigan," paper presented at the meeting of the American Alliance for Health, Recreation, Physical Education, and Dance, Kansas City, Missouri, 1978.

Page 20. The survey of children who had recently stopped playing a sport is from the report "American Youth and Sports Participation" (North Palm Beach, Fla.: Athletic Footwear Association, 1990). The 2,700 boys and 3,100 girls surveyed were in grades seven through twelve.

Page 21. The study of 695 male and female college athletes concerning eating disorders was by Burckes-Miller, M. E., and Black, D. R., "Male and Female College Athletes: Prevalence of Anorexia Nervosa and Bulimia Nervosa," *Athletic Training*, 1988, *23*, 137–140.

Page 22. Some estimates of the prevalence of injury problems in youth sports are provided in Micheli, L., *SportsWise: An Essential Guide for Young Athletes, Parents, and Coaches* (Boston, Mass.: Houghton Mifflin, 1990).

Page 23. The recent survey of 965 students at four Massachusetts middle schools was by Faigenbaum, A., Zaichkowsky, L., Gardner, D. Michelil, L., "Anabolic steroid use by male and female middle school students," *Pediatrics*, May 1997, 101 (5), e1–e6.

Page 24. The study of intercollegiate athletes was conducted by Wechsler, H., and colleagues, "Correlates of College Student Binge Drinking," *American Journal of Public Health*, 1995, *85*, 921–926.

Page 24. Carr, C. M., Kennedy, S. R., and Dimick, K. M., "Alcohol Use and Abuse Among High School Athletes: A Comparison of Alcohol Use and Intoxication in Male and Female High School Athletes and Nonathletes," *Journal of Alcohol and Drug Education*, 1990, *36*, 39–45.

Page 24. The quote from University of Winnipeg sociologist Sandra Kirby is from Allen, K., "'Dome of Silence' Often Shrouds Truth," *USA Today*, Jan. 6, 1997, p. 3C.

Chapter Two

Page 30. The quote from the resolution advising school personnel not to organize competitive sports programs for grade-school-age children is from "Two

Important Resolutions," *Journal of Health and Physical Education*, 1938, 9, 448–489. Quoted in Berryman, J. W., "The Rise of Boys' Sports in the United States, 1900 to 1970," in F. L. Smoll and R. E. Smith (eds.), *Children and Youth in Sport: A Biopsychological Perspective* (Madison, Wis.: Brown & Benchmark, 1996), p. 7.

Pages 30. Historical information on the development of youth sports programs comes from the following articles: Berryman, J. W., "The Rise of Boys' Sports in the United States, 1900 to 1970," in F. L. Smoll and R. E. Smith (eds.), *Children and Youth in Sport: A Biopsychosocial Perspective* (Madison, Wis.: Brown & Benchmark, 1996), pp. 4–14; Wiggins, D. K., "A History of Highly Competitive Sport for American Children," in Smoll and Smith, pp. 15–30; Wiggins, D. K., "A History of Organized Play and Highly Competitive Sport for American Children," in D. Gould and M. Weiss (eds.), *Advances in Pediatric Sport Sciences*, Vol. 2: *Behavioral Issues* (Champaign, Ill.: Human Kinetics, 1987), pp. 1–25.

Page 31. The statistics on the number of children involved in youth sports and their level of involvement are drawn from Gould, D., "Understanding Attrition in Children's Sports," in D. Gould and M. Weiss (eds.), *Advances in Pediatric Sport Sciences*, Vol. 2: *Behavioral Issues* (Champaign, Ill.: Human Kinetics, 1987), pp. 61–86, and Weinberg, R.S. and Gould, D., "Children's Psychological Development Through Sport," in J. Silva and R. Weinberg (eds.), *Foundations of Sport and Exercise Psychology* (Champaign, Ill.: Human Kinetics, 1987), pp. 449–466.

Page 32. Figures on the business of sports are drawn from Rosner, D., "The World Plays Catch-Up," *SportsInc*, Jan. 2, 1989, pp. 6–13.

Page 34. Coakley, J., *Sport in Society: Issues and Controversies* (6th ed.) (Boston: McGraw-Hill, 1998), pp. 337–338.

Chapter Three

Page 43. The issue of parents being expected to know where their child is at all times is discussed in Coakley, J., *Sport in Society: Issues and Controversies* (6th ed.) (Boston: McGraw-Hill, 1998), p. 118.

Page 46. The research that shows that young people who are active in sports programs tend to benefit in a wide range of related areas includes such studies as Segrave, J., and Chu, D., "Athletics and Juvenile Delinquency," *Review of Sport and Leisure*, 1978, 3, pp. 1–24.

Chapter Four

Page 60. Research on the variety of motives expressed by children for playing sports is summarized in Gould, D., and Horn, T., "Participation Motivation in Young Athletes," in J. Silva and R. Weinberg (eds.), *Foundations of Sport and Exercise Psychology* (Champaign, Ill.: Human Kinetics, 1987), pp. 359–370.

Page 60. The theory of flow is described in Csikszentmihalyi, M., *Flow: The Psychology of Optimal Experience* (New York: HarperCollins, 1990).

Page 61. Surveys that asked children why they stopped playing sports are summarized in Weiss, M.R., and Petlichkoff, L.M., "Children's Motivation for Participation in and Withdrawal from Sport: Identifying the Missing Links," *Pediatric Exercise Science*, 1989, *I*, 195–211.

Page 65. The video *Two Ball Games* can be ordered in VHS format for $150 from Department of Psychology, 208 Uris Hall, Cornell University, Ithaca, NY 14853.

Page 66. The observations on informal play are provided in Coakley, J., "Children and the Sport Socialization Process," in D. Gould and M. Weiss (eds.), *Advances in Pediatric Sport Sciences* (Vol. 2) (Champaign, Ill.: Human Kinetics, 1987), pp. 43–60.

Page 72. Research demonstrating the influence of the coach on children's satisfaction can be found in Smith, R., Smoll, F., and Curtis, B., "Coaching Behaviors in Little League Baseball," in Smoll, F., and Smith, R. (eds.), *Psychological Perspectives in Youth Sports* (Bristol, Pa.: Hemisphere, 1978).

Page 75. Research on competition and anxiety is summarized in Smoll, F., and Smith, R., "Competitive Anxiety: Sources, Consequences, and Intervention Strategies," in F. Smoll and R. Smith, *Children and Youth in Sport: A Biopsychological Perspective* (Madison, Wis.: Brown & Benchmark, 1996).

Chapter Five

Page 83. The advice often given to parents is from Fine, A. H., and Sachs, M. L., "The Total Sports Experience for Kids: A Parents' Guide to Success in Youth Sports" (South Bend, Ind.: Diamond Communications, 1997), p. 148.

Page 91. Cognitive therapy is described by Beck, A.T., *Cognitive Therapy and the Emotional Disorders* (New York: Meridian, 1975).

Page 92. The concept of the central paradox comes from Hellstedt, J., "Invisible Players," in S. Murphy (ed.), *Sport Psychology Interventions* (Champaign, Ill.: Human Kinetics, 1995).

Page 93. The research project I conducted with Othon Kesend is described in his manuscript, "The Motivation of Elite Athletes: A Developmental Perspective," submitted to The Union Institute, 1991.

Page 94. The study of baseball players is reported in Hill, G., "Youth Sport Participation of Professional Baseball Players," *Sociology of Sport Journal*, 1993, *10*, 107–114.

Page 95. Kohn, A., *No Contest: The Case Against Competition* (Boston: Houghton Mifflin, 1992), pp. 91–92.

Chapter Six

Page 110. Several long-term research projects on young people who display excellence at an early age are summarized in Bloom, B., *Developing Talent in Young People* (New York: Ballantine Books, 1985). Specific research into the characteristics of the families of these talented young people is described in a chapter by K. Sloane, "Home Influences on Talent Development," pp. 439–476.

Page 114. The study of former elite figure skaters was reported in Scanlan, T., Stein, G., and Ravizza. K., "An In-Depth Study of Former Elite Figure Skaters: II. Sources of Enjoyment," *The Journal of Sport and Exercise Psychology*, 1989, *11*, 65–83. The quote is from pp. 75–76.

Page 115. The ideas of Steven Danish concerning personal competence are described in the chapter "Psychological interventions: A life development model," by Steven Danish, Al Petitpas, and Bruce Hale, in S. Murphy (Ed.), *Sport psychology interventions* (Champaign, Ill: Human Kinetics, 1995, p.23).

Page 116. The model of stages of development for the typical athletic family is explained in Hellstedt, J., "Invisible Players," in S. Murphy (ed.), *Sport Psychology Interventions* (Champaign, Ill.: Human Kinetics, 1995).

Page 123. The research on adolescent athletes who had been age-group champions but had quit is described in Coakley, J., "Burnout Among Adolescent Athletes: A Personal Failure or Social Problem?" *Sociology of Sport Journal*, 1992, *9*, pp. 271–285.

Chapter Seven

Page 139. The concepts of ego orientation and mastery orientation are described in Nicholls, J., *The Competitive Ethos and Democratic Education* (Cambridge, Mass.: Harvard University Press, 1989), pp. 95–97.

Page 139. These ideas on ego and mastery orientations are drawn from my experience and from such research as Duda, J., "The Relationship Between Goal Perspectives, Persistence, and Behavioral Intensity Among Male and Female Recreational Sport Participants," *Leisure Sciences*, 1988, *10*, 95–106. Duda found that among intramural college athletes, the high ego/low mastery group reported the least amount of practice time.

Page 142. Glyn Roberts and his colleagues suggest that the most at-risk athletes for developing motivation problems are high ego, low mastery athletes. Roberts, G., Treasure, D., and Kavussanu, M., "Othogonality of Achievement Goals and Its Relationship to Beliefs About Success and Satisfaction in Sport," *The Sport Psychologist*, 1996, *10*, 398–408.

Page 146. The research underlying the concept of the differentiation of effort and ability is described in Nicholls, J., *The Competitive Ethos and Democratic Education* (Cambridge, Mass.: Harvard University Press, 1989).

Page 149. The research on motivational climate is described in Duda, J.L., "Maximizing Motivation in Sport and Physical Education Among Children and Adolescents: The Case for Greater Task Involvement," *Quest*, 1996, *48*, 290–302.

Page 152. How to set effective goals is a topic I have tackled in depth in one of my previous books, *The Achievement Zone* (New York: Berkley, 1997). In Chapter 1 (pp. 21–47), on action focus, I discuss in detail the differences between focusing on results and focusing on how to achieve results.

Page 155. Coach Effectiveness Training is described in *Way to Go, Coach!* (Portola Valley, CA: Warde Publishers, 1996). Phone: (800) 699-2733.

Chapter Eight

Page 161. Ryan, J., *Little Girls in Pretty Boxes: The Making and Breaking of Elite Gymnasts and Figure Skaters* (New York: Warner Books, 1995), p. 238.

Page 162. Kohn, A., *No Contest: The Case Against Competition* (Boston: Houghton Mifflin, 1992).

Page 163. Triplett, N.L., "Dynamogenic Factors in Pacemaking and Competition," *American Journal of Psychology*, 1898, 9, 507–533.

Page 164. Gardner, H., *Creating Minds* (New York: Basic Books, 1993), p. 36.

Page 165. The research on the development of self-esteem in young athletes is described in Weiss, M., "Children in Sport," in S. Murphy (ed.), *Sport Psychology Interventions* (Champaign, Ill.: Human Kinetics, 1995).

Page 167. The research on why children play youth sports was conducted by Scanlan, T., Stein, G., and Ravizza, K., "An In-Depth Study of Former Elite Figure Skaters. II: Sources of Enjoyment," *Journal of Sport and Exercise Psychology,* 1989, 11, 65–83.

Page 167. The research on the development and prevention of competitive anxiety in young athletes is described in Smoll, F., and Smith, R., "Competitive Anxiety: Sources, Consequences, and Intervention Strategies," in F. Smoll and R. Smith, *Children and Youth in Sport: A Biopsychological Perspective* (Madison, Wis.: Brown & Benchmark, 1996).

Page 168. Csikszentmihalyi, M., *Flow: The Psychology of Optimal Experience* (New York: HarperCollins, 1990).

Page 170. Research findings on problems such as eating disorders and alcoholism are found in Murphy, S.M. (ed.), *Sport Psychology Interventions* (Champaign, Ill: Human Kinetics, 1995).

Page 170. Research in the moral development of young athletes is found in Bredemeier, B.J., and Shields, D.L., "Moral Growth Through Physical Activity: A Structural/Developmental Approach," in D. Gould and M. Weiss (eds.),

Advances in Pediatric Sport Sciences, Vol. 2: *Behavioral Issues* (Champaign, Ill.: Human Kinetics, 1987), pp. 143–165.

Page 171. The findings on the values of the young athlete were described by Beller, J., "Helping Female Athletes Develop Character On and Off the Field," a workshop presented at the Powerful Coaching: Beyond X's and O's conference. Smith College, Massachusetts, 1998.

Page 173. In fact, I have found that elite athletes are not extraordinarily ego oriented. Most have a high mastery orientation as well. It often seems that professional sports are driven by a high ego orientation because they are covered that way by the media. In fact, it is the sports media that have the high ego orientation, not the athletes.

Page 173. The findings on the high rates of athletes with eating problems is described in Brownell, K.D. and Rodin, J., "Prevalence of Eating Disorders in Athletes," in K.D. Brownell, J. Rodin, and J.H. Wilmore (eds.), *Eating, Body Weight, and Performance in Athletes* (Malvern, Penn.: Lea & Fabiger, 1992), pp. 128–145.

Page 174. Carr, C. M., Kennedy, S. R., and Dimick, K. M., "Alcohol Use and Abuse Among High School Athletes: A Comparison of Alcohol Use and Intoxication in Male and Female High School Athletes and Nonathletes," *Journal of Alcohol and Drug Education,* 1990, 36, 39–45.

Page 179. From Orlick, T., and Zitzelsberger, L., "Enhancing Children's Sport Experiences," in F. Smoll and R. Smith (eds.), *Children and Youth Sport: A Biopsychological Perspective* (Madison, Wis.: Brown & Benchmark, 1996), pp. 330–337.

Page 179. For an overview of the work on emotional intelligence, see Goleman, D., *Emotional Intelligence* (New York: Bantam Books, 1995).

Chapter Nine

Page 192. For more information on the American Youth Soccer Organization (AYSO), contact: (800)˙872-2976.

Page 196. The A Sporting Chance Foundation program and many other wonderful sports programs for girls are described in Greenberg, D. (ed.), *Sports in the Lives of Urban Girls: A Resource Manual for Girls' Sports in Urban Areas* (Women's Sports Foundation, 1998. Phone: (800) 227–3988.

FOR FURTHER READING

Several excellent books are available for parents, coaches, and administrators who are interested in how to put together great youth sports programs, and how to maximize the benefits of such programs. For parents, I recommend the following:

The Total Sports Experience for Kids: A Parents' Guide to Success in Youth Sports, by Aubrey Fine and Michael Sachs. South Bend, Ind.: Diamond Communications, 1997.

A terrific book for coaches of children is

Way to Go, Coach! by Ron Smith and Frank Smoll. Portola Valley, Calif.: Warde Publishers, 1996.

And for children I recommend

Christy's Magic Glove, by Gibb Davis. New York: Bantam Skylark Books, 1992. (For young children.)
In These Girls, Hope Is a Muscle, by Madeline Blais. New York: Atlantic Monthly Press, 1995. (For older children.)

Good books on sport psychology and the psychology of performance and excellence include

In Pursuit of Excellence (2nd ed.), by Terry Orlick. Champaign, Ill: Human
    Kinetics, 1990.
Athletic Excellence: Mental Toughness Training for Sports, by Jim Loehr and E. J.
    Kahn. Denver, Colo.: Forum Publishing, 1987.
Flow: The Psychology of Optimal Experience, by Mihaly Csikszentmihalyi.
    New York: HarperCollins, 1992.

For those who wish to study this topic in greater detail, I highly recommend

Children and Youth in Sport: A Biopsychosocial Perspective, by Frank Smoll and
    Ron Smith. Madison, Wis.: Brown & Benchmark, 1996.
Sport in Society: Issues and Controversies (6th ed.), by Jay Coakley. Boston:
    McGraw-Hill, 1998.
*Sports in the Lives of Urban Girls: A Resource Manual for Girls' Sports in Urban
    Areas*, edited by Doreen Greenberg. Los Angeles, CA: Women's Sports
    Foundation, 1998. (Phone: (800) 227–3988).

And for some sobering reading on the dark side of youth sports programs, I suggest

*Little Girls in Pretty Boxes: The Making and Breaking of Elite Gymnasts and Figure
    Skaters*, by Joan Ryan. New York: Warner Books, 1995.
Inside Edge: A Revealing Journey into the Secret World of Figure Skating, by Chris-
    tine Brennan. New York: Scribner, 1996.
Ladies of the Court: Grace and Disgrace on the Women's Tennis Tour, by Michael
    Mewshaw. New York: Warner Books, 1993.

Finally, the influence of gender issues on sports participation has
been cogently analyzed in

"Gender Issues: A Social-Educational Perspective," by Diane Gill. In S. Murphy
    (ed.), *Sport Psychology Interventions*. Champaign, Ill: Human Kinetics,
    1995, pp. 205–234.
"Gender: Is Equity the Only Issue?" by Jay Coakley. In J. Coakley (ed.), *Sport in
    Society: Issues and Controversies* (6th ed.). Boston: McGraw-Hill, 1997,
    pp. 210–247.

"Sport Socialization," by Susan Greendorfer. In T. Horn (ed.), *Advances in Sport Psychology*. Champaign, Ill.: Human Kinetics, 1992, pp. 201–218.

Eating, Body Weight, and Performance in Athletes, by Kelly Brownell, Judith Rodin, and Jack Willmore. Malvern, Pa.: Lea & Febiger, 1992.

FOR MORE INFORMATION

For parents who would like to explore options in youth sports programs, there are many alternatives beyond the traditional American youth sports, such as baseball, soccer, gymnastics, basketball, and ice hockey. The following is a list of contact information for a variety of sports organizations. These organizations can help you find available youth sports programs in your area or provide you with more information on sports for children.

MULTISPORT ORGANIZATIONS

American Alliance for Health,
Recreation, Physical
Education and Dance
1900 Association Drive
Reston, VA 22091
(703) 476-3400

Boys and Girls Clubs
of America
1230 West Peach Street, NW
Atlanta, GA 30309
(404) 815-5700
www.bgca.org

Catholic Youth Organization
(CYO)
1011 First Avenue, Room 620
New York, NY, 10022
(212) 371-1000, ext. 2064

Disabled Sports USA
451 Hungerford Drive,
Suite 100
Rockville, MD 20850
(301) 217-0960

National Alliance
for Youth Sports
2050 Vista Parkway
West Palm Beach, FL 33411
(561) 684-1141
www.nays.org

National Association of Police
Athletic Leagues
618 North U.S. Highway 1,
Suite 201
North Palm Beach, FL 33408
(407) 844-1823

President's Council on Physical
Fitness and Sports
200 Independence Avenue,
SW
HHH Building, Room 738-H
Washington, DC 20201
(202) 690-9000
www.indiana.edu/~preschal

Special Olympics International
1325 G Street, NW, Suite 500
Washington, DC 20005
(202) 628-3630

Wheelchair Sports USA
3595 East Fountain Boulevard,
Suite L-1
Colorado Springs, CO 80910
(719) 574-1150

Young Men's Christian
Association (YMCA)
101 North Wacker Drive
Chicago, IL 60606
(312) 977-0031

Young Women's Christian
Association (YWCA)
Empire State Building,
Suite 301
350 Fifth Avenue
New York, NY 10118
Phone: (212) 273-7800

SPORT ORGANIZATIONS

National Archery Association
One Olympic Plaza
Colorado Springs, CO 80909
(719) 578-4576

U.S. Badminton Association
One Olympic Plaza
Colorado Springs, CO 80909
(719) 578-4808

U.S. Biathlon Association
421 Old Military Road
Lake Placid, NY 12946
(518) 523-3836

U.S. Bobsled and Skeleton
Federation
P.O. Box 828,
421 Old Military Road

Lake Placid, NY 12946
(518) 523-1842

USA Bowling
5301 South 76th Street
Greendale, WI 53129-0500
(414) 421-9008

U.S. Canoe and Kayak Team
(USCKT)
P.O. Box 789
Lake Placid, NY 12946
(518) 523-1855

USA Curling
1100 Center Point Drive
(P.O. Box 866)
Stevens Point, WI 54481
(715) 344-1199

USA Cycling
One Olympic Plaza
Colorado Springs, CO 80909
(719) 578-4581

United States Diving
Pan American Plaza,
Suite 430201
South Capitol Avenue
Indianapolis, IN 46225
(317) 237-5252

U.S. Fencing Association
One Olympic Plaza
Colorado Springs, CO 80909
(719) 578-4511

U.S. Field Hockey
Association
1520 N. Union Blvd.
Colorado Springs, CO 80909
(719) 578-4567

United States Judo
P.O. Box 10013
El Paso, TX 79991
(915) 771-6699

U.S. Luge Association
P.O. Box 651
(35 Church Street)
Lake Placid, NY 12946
(518) 523-2071

U.S. Orienteering
Federation
P.O. Box 1444
Forest Park, GA 30051
(404) 363-2110

American Amateur
Racquetball Association
1685 West Uintah
Colorado Springs, CO 80904
(719) 635-5396

U.S. Rowing Association
Pan American Plaza,
Suite 400201
South Capitol Avenue
Indianapolis, IN 46225
(317) 237-5656

U.S. Sailing
P.O. Box 1260
(15 Maritime Drive)
Newport, RI 02871-0924
(401) 683-0800

U.S. Speedskating
P.O. Box 16157
Rocky River, OH 44116
(216) 899-0128

U.S. Squash Racquets
Association
P.O. Box 1216
Bala Cynwyd, PA 19004
(610) 667-4006

United States Sports
Acrobatics Federation
P.O. Box 8158
Riverside, CA 92515-8158
(909) 785-2293

U.S. Synchronized Swimming
Pan American Plaza,
Suite 510201
South Capitol Avenue
Indianapolis, IN 46225
(317) 237-5700

USA Table Tennis
One Olympic Plaza
Colorado Springs, CO 80909
(719) 578-4583

U.S. Taekwondo Union
One Olympic Plaza
Colorado Springs, CO 80909
(719) 578-4632

U.S. Team Handball
Federation
One Olympic Plaza
Colorado Springs, CO
80909-5768
(719) 578-4582

U.S. Tennis Association
70 West Red Oak Lane
White Plains, NY 10604-3602
(914) 696-7000

USA Track and Field
P.O. Box 120
(1 Hoosier Dome, Suite 140)
Indianapolis, IN 46206
(317) 261-0500

USA Trampoline and Tumbling
P.O. Box 306
Brownfield, TX 79316-0306
(806) 637-8670

Triathlon Federation USA
3595 East Fountain Boulevard,
Suite F-1
Colorado Springs, CO
80910-1740
(719) 597-9090

USA Volleyball
3595 East Fountain Boulevard,
Suite I-2
Colorado Springs, CO
80910-1740
(719) 637-8300

United States Water Polo
Pan American Plaza,
Suite 520201
South Capitol Avenue
Indianapolis, IN 46225
(317) 237-5599

American Water Ski
Federation
799 Overlook Drive, SE
Winter Haven, FL 33884
(813) 324-4341

U.S. Weightlifting
One Olympic Plaza
Colorado Springs, CO
80909-5764
(719) 578-4508

USA Wrestling
6155 Lehman Drive
Colorado Springs, CO 80918
(719) 598-8181

ABOUT THE AUTHOR

Shane Murphy is a leader in the field of sport psychology. From 1987 to 1994 he was the chief sport psychologist for the United States Olympic Committee in Colorado Springs. He was the USA team psychologist at the 1988 Summer Games in Seoul and at the 1992 Winter Games in Albertville. He was also the sport psychology consultant with the USA Whitewater Canoe/Kayak team at the Olympics in Atlanta in 1996.

Murphy has counseled athletes in more than forty-five different sports, including extensive experience with top athletes in sports as diverse as figure skating, track and field, archery, kayaking, tennis, speed skating, judo, boxing, golf, soccer, and cycling. He works with many young athletes, and both his children participate in sports.

He edited the book *Sport Psychology Interventions,* published in 1995, and wrote the book *The Achievement Zone: An Eight-Step Guide to Peak Performance in All Arenas of Life,* published in 1997. It has been translated into Japanese, Chinese, and German.

Murphy is president of the Division of Sport and Exercise Psychology of the American Psychological Association. He is a popular speaker on youth sports issues, and through his consulting firm, Gold Medal Psychological Consultants, provides consultation on performance issues to sport teams, school districts, athletes, coaches, and companies. He lives in Connecticut with his wife, Annemarie, and their two children.

INDEX